GREAT DRAWINGS
AND ILLUSTRATIONS FROM
PUNCH
1841-1901

VARNISHING DAY AT THE ROYAL ACADEMY.

George du Maurier, 5–19–77

GREAT DRAWINGS AND ILLUSTRATIONS FROM PUNCH

1841-1901

192 Works by
Leech, Keene, du Maurier, May
and 21 Others

Edited by
Stanley Appelbaum & Richard Kelly

DOVER PUBLICATIONS, INC., NEW YORK

Published in Canada by General Publishing Company, Ltd., 30 Lesmill Road, Don Mills, Toronto, Ontario.
Published in the United Kingdom by Constable and Company, Ltd., 10 Orange Street, London WC2H 7EG.

Great Drawings and Illustrations from Punch, *1841–1901: 192 Works by Leech, Keene, du Maurier, May and 21 Others* is a new work, first published by Dover Publications, Inc., in 1981.

International Standard Book Number: 0-486-24110-6
Library of Congress Catalog Card Number: 80-70186

Manufactured in the United States of America
Dover Publications, Inc.
180 Varick Street
New York, N.Y. 10014

CONTENTS

PREFACE

Anthologies of drawings from *Punch* have already been published from many points of view, and others surely will be, for the magazine is an endless quarry of accomplished art. Although it is hoped that a great number of the selections herein will be found both amusing and instructive to the social historian, the overriding criteria for inclusion in the present volume were excellence of draftsmanship and pictorial interest.

The period covered is 1841–1901. Not only is this a fine round number of 60 years from the inception of the magazine; 1901 also marks the death of Queen Victoria and the retirement of Tenniel, doubly the end of an era. The selection has been made from the regular weekly issues and from the annual Almanacks (always so spelled; the Almanack for each year appeared early in December of the preceding year). Small vignettes, headpieces and the like have not been included.

The artists are presented (in the picture pages and in the biographical section) in alphabetical order. In certain instances it has seemed preferable to list them by their better-known pseudonyms (all pseudonyms in the volume appear within quotation marks). In the biographical literature there are discrepancies in the form of certain names. The small "d" used here for George du Maurier is based on his actual signature. Our "Raven-Hill, Leonard" (as opposed to "Hill, Leonard Raven") is based on *Who Was Who* and other standard references. Within each artist's work, the sequence is basically chronological.

Most of the drawings are furnished with the dates of the issues from which they were chosen, in the form "10–3–96," standing for "October 3, 1896." Before the mid-1850s, however, the issues were not dated, and a different form of reference is thus adopted here: "Jan.–Jun. '42, p. 66," standing for "page 66 of the volume consisting of the months January through June of 1842."

INTRODUCTION

"For more than half a century, *Punch* has been a school of wood-drawing, of pen and pencil draughtsmanship, and of wood-cutting of the first rank; it is a school of art in itself."
— MARION HARRY SPIELMANN, 1895

One of the most long-lived of periodicals and still a welcome treat to thousands of Englishmen and Anglophiles — though perhaps no longer a molder of British opinion — *Punch* stood out from among its many rivals at its inception by being exceptionally clean for a humor magazine and exceptionally sharp for a political combatant. Its longevity, however, could only have been achieved by making it a habit with the consumer, an unofficial national institution that avoided sectional strife and the giving of offense — at least to its normal customers, the educated and would-be educated upper and middle classes. This pacific goal had been largely attained by the 1860s (no longer, as in the early 1850s, would a Richard Doyle be driven off the Staff by anti-Catholic jibes, or a Thackeray by unbridled attacks on Louis-Napoléon), and was an accomplished fact by the end of the century.

By the late 1800s the magazine was such a phenomenal success that acrid and confusing controversy over the true history of its founding was rife. It is fairly clear, however, that when the first issue of *Punch; or The London Charivari* (the subtitle being a bow to its illustrious Parisian predecessor, Charles Philipon's *Charivari*) appeared on July 17, 1841, the management consisted of the printer Ebenezer Landells, a publisher named Bryant and a brain trust headed by Henry Mayhew, Mark Lemon and Joseph Stirling Coyne. In a matter of a year, dire financial difficulties, alleviated but not eliminated by the issuance of the first annual Almanack, caused a reorganization in which Landells and Bryant were squeezed out, and both the publishing and the printing were assumed by the solid and businesslike — though far from unimaginative — firm of Bradbury & Evans.

Artwork was definitely secondary to letterpress in the earliest years, and indeed *Punch* was fortunate in the nineteenth century to have such writers as William Thackeray, Douglas Jerrold, Thomas Hood ("The Song of the Shirt" appeared in the outspokenly liberal *Punch* of 1843), Andrew Lang, Coventry Patmore and Alfred Tennyson, not to mention its own capable editors, including Lemon, Shirley Brooks and Francis Cowley Burnand. But between 1855 and 1865 the proportion of artists to writers on the Staff slowly increased until the former group was preponderant. Needless to say, the drawings, more accessible to us today, are the best remembered and most vital aspect of nineteenth-century *Punch*.

Artistic standards on the magazine were not yet high in the 1840s, and really well-drawn pictures (by almost any criterion) are exceptions in that decade. In the first three years or so (1841–1844), Hablôt Knight Browne ("Phiz") was best of all, though he did not appear regularly enough to give the magazine any kind of cachet; while Kenny Meadows and "Alfred Crowquill" (Alfred Henry Forrester) were interesting and talented holdovers from an earlier, more primitive state of humorous art. For the remainder of the 1840s, Richard Doyle, especially in his vignettes, was a highly characteristic *Punch* artist, but exuding a fragile charm rather than impressing with sureness of touch. The real draftsman-champion of the first decade — and proceeding erratically from strength to strength until his untimely death in 1864 — was the great illustrator John Leech, the first of the half-dozen (or fewer) artistic pillars of the magazine in the nineteenth century.

The 1850s — aside from the acquisition in those years of two more "pillars," John Tenniel and Charles Keene, who had not yet hit their full stride — were not appreciably better in artwork than the 1840s. It was with the 1860s, a renaissance era for British illustration in general and the beginning of quieter gentility for *Punch*, that the magazine really blossomed out artistically. Not only did Tenniel and Keene then become the institutions they would remain until late in the century (and Keene one of the most extravagantly praised, though officially little recognized, British artists of his day); but also the brilliant and suave George du Maurier began his 35-year association with the magazine, linking his name with it indissolubly. There was also room in the 1860s for cheerful oddities like Ernest Griset.

The 1870s and 1880s were years of dignified prosperity in *Punch's* art. During this time Linley Sambourne moved up quickly from small eccentricities to astonishingly exuberant and fantasy-filled pages, in which he sometimes left all competitors far behind. A. Chantrey Corbould and many other comfortably accomplished draftsmen helped make *Punch* truly the "school of art" of which the magazine's historian Spielmann spoke. From 1884 on, Harry Furniss points the way to the new, in many ways loftier, plateau of the 1890s.

The years from 1890 to 1901 (the upper limit of this survey) are rich in experiment and achievement. Men like Alexander Boyd and Reginald Cleaver introduce a newer sort of journalistic draftsmanship. Bernard Partridge brings an up-to-date brand of academicism; C. E. Brock, an easy-going new illustrative style; and E. T. Reed, a kind of "goofy" treatment that leads right into twentieth-century developments. Perhaps the most important group in the 1890s are Phil May, Leonard Raven-Hill and Dudley Hardy, with their new loosening and lessening of line and their more democratic outlook.

Throughout the Victorian era, *Punch* was also glad to welcome a number of infrequently contributing guest artists of the highest caliber, among whom "Cham," John Everett Millais, Fred Walker, Randolph Caldecott and "Caran d'Ache" are represented in this volume.

In order to avoid obscurity or endless historical explanations, the present selection of drawings includes very few examples of a class of art that has always been of extreme importance to *Punch:* the "cartoons."* This term, which denotes the large-scale political drawings, of which usually one or two appeared each week, came into use in 1843, when the Houses of Parliament were being decorated by murals (Tenniel, the *Punch*

---

*In the present volume, "cartoon" will appear within quotation marks when used with its special meaning.

"cartoonist" par excellence in the period under review, did one). "Cartoon," deriving from the Italian *cartone* ("large sheet of paper"), was and is the traditional term for a large, finished preliminary drawing for some monumental work of art such as a fresco or a tapestry. There was so much talk in 1843 about the cartoons for Parliament that *Punch* jocularly adopted the word for its major political drawings. The designation "cartoon" was never applied to any other kind of *Punch* drawing in the nineteenth century and, despite strong leveling influence from America, where the term became more generalized, it still basically bears its older meaning in England today.

Punch "cartoons" were carefully studied at home and abroad by those concerned with the way the political wind was blowing. To decide on the subject and handling of the next "cartoon" was one of the essential purposes of the weekly dinners at *Punch's* very exclusive Table, a gathering of editors, representatives of Bradbury & Evans, literary and artistic contributors and various specialized advisers. Of about 170 artists who had drawn for *Punch* by 1895, fewer than twenty had been invited to the august decision-making Table.

Punch (once it outgrew its stormy beginnings) could be highly conservative, not to say backward, in a number of ways. For almost the entire Victorian era, its chief method of reproducing its drawings was wood engraving—and this long after other periodicals had moved on to newer techniques. A late eighteenth-century development, "white-line" wood engraving (as opposed to the medieval and Renaissance "black-line" woodcut) at first called for the actual drawing to be done by the artist on the wood block, which would then be incised by the wood engraver, a separate specialist (*Punch's* chief engraver from 1843 to his death in 1890 was the superb craftsman Joseph Swain). The finished wood block was locked up with the type, and text and pictures printed together. Later, it was possible to transfer the drawings onto the block by the use of transfer paper or—beginning in the 1850s, but not in general use until the 1870s—photographically. The *Punch* "cartoons," the most sacrosanct category of artwork, were drawn directly on the wood until 1892.

In the 1840s some publications abandoned the traditional single wood block per drawing for the use of six wood sections per drawing screwed or bolted into one master block. This system, which allowed more than one engraver to work on a drawing at once, was a boon to journalists with deadlines and helped change wood engraving from a craft into an industry. *Punch*, however, continued to use single blocks until about 1860.

Some artists and connoisseurs complained occasionally that the wood engravers had spoiled the original conceptions and that only the original pen or pencil drawings showed the work in its pure and true state. Yet, the drawings were commissioned to be reproduced, and the artists themselves were often at fault for preparing their art in a less than professional way, no matter how "beautifully." Often, too, the wood engraver was blamed for a smudgy finished product that was really the result of using relatively unrefined rapid cylinder presses on very big printing runs.

Known in some form from the 1860s, perfected in the 1870s and in general use in the 1880s, the next important reproductive method was stereotyping, or "process," in which the original drawing was photographed onto a metal plate that was then bitten with acid—an industrial branch of fine-art etching which allowed great fidelity in reproducing original pen work and changed the look of most magazine art. *Punch* did not use this technique until the end of 1892, and the sacred chief "cartoon" was still printed by wood block until 1900!

Nor was it until well into the twentieth century, largely under competitive pressure from *The New Yorker*, that the captions ("legends") of *Punch* drawings were strongly curtailed. By the 1890s, Phil May and likeminded "modernists" were shortening them appreciably—but only by the standards of the time. During the late nineteenth century, *Punch* even printed a few humorous drawings without text, but these were always ponderously labeled as such. Nevertheless, when reading these long, involved texts, whose wit does not reside in brevity, it is possible to take a less teleological view (why assume that everything today is perfect and everything older was merely a fumbling approximation?), and to appreciate the fine ear for speech patterns and dialect, as well as the now vanished erudition, that grace some of the finest examples.

THE ARTISTS

Alexander Stuart Boyd [1854–1930; pages 1 & 2]. Not one of the giants of *Punch* history, Boyd is nevertheless a delightful representative of the numerous minor but excellently trained artists who helped fill the pages of the magazine during the 1890s, a particularly felicitous period in English illustration. Along with Reginald Cleaver and others, he also represents a group of art contributors to *Punch* at this time whose technique had been formed at least partially by journalistic experience on the highly successful *Daily Graphic*.

Born in Glasgow, Boyd (also a painter specializing in landscapes) began magazine work in his native city, contributing under the name of "Twym" to the journals *Quiz* and *The Bailie*. Drawings by Boyd for these publications were gathered into book form in 1905 as *Glasgow Men and Women*. Joining *Punch* in 1894, Boyd also contributed in the 1890s to *Good Words* and *The Idler*. He illustrated Israel Zangwill's *Ghetto Tragedies* (1894), as well as books by Bret Harte, Jerome K. Jerome and various Scottish authors.

Charles Edmund Brock [1870–1938; page 3]. C. E. Brock is of course best known as the illustrator of a host of English classics, including Hood, Swift, Lamb, Thackeray and Austen, to name just a few. Influenced by Hugh Thomson and Randolph Caldecott, his style was somewhat rougher than theirs, and he gained fame as a direct and unmannered draftsman, especially good at period costumes and settings.

Without formal art training, Brock did study for a while with the Cambridge sculptor Henry Wiles. In that university town, Brock shared a garden studio with his three younger brothers, the most celebrated of whom was the illustrator H. M. (Henry Matthew) Brock. C. E. Brock's work for *Punch* begins at the very end of the Victorian era (the time frame of this volume); in the 1890s and 1900s he also drew for *The Graphics* and *Good Words*.

Hablôt Knight Browne ["Phiz"; 1815–1882; page 4]. Born in the London area, Browne studied copper engraving and painting (the latter with William Etty) and did some architectural drawing before making his great name as the chief illustrator of Dickens for over two decades. It was in 1836, when Browne succeeded the unfortunate Robert Seymour as illustrator of *Pickwick*, that he discarded his earlier pseudonym "Nemo" for the now famous one that matched Dickens' "Boz." Other major authors illustrated by Browne were Byron, Scott, Lever and Ainsworth. Despite his great reputation, Browne has had severe critics, who blame him especially for being unoriginal, repetitious and far too rowdy in his comic scenes.

Browne, who designed the second of *Punch's* several standard covers, contributed to the magazine from 1842 to 1844, when, ousted by competition from Leech, he left to become leading artist of *The Great Gun* (he also worked for *Judy*). Only sporadic odds and ends by Browne appeared in *Punch* thereafter. The Browne item reproduced here was one of a set of humorous valentines drawn by several contributors early in 1842; it is one of the very best drawings in the pages of *Punch* in the rather mediocre 1840s and 1850s.

Randolph Caldecott [1846–1886; pages 5 & 6]. Only a very occasional contributor to *Punch*, Caldecott — whose name lives on in the coveted prize for illustrators of juveniles — is best remembered as one of the revolutionizers of children's books. Between 1878 and 1885, replacing Walter Crane, he produced sixteen timeless picture stories for the outstanding color printer Edmund Evans. But Caldecott was also active as a black-and-white and color contributor to numerous publications, including *The Illustrated London News* (as early as 1861!), *London Society*, *The Will-o'-the-Wisp*, *The Sphinx*, *The Pictorial World* and especially *The Graphic*. He was also a sort of travel reporter, much of the travel being to warm places and necessitated by his tubercular condition (see the "Ironical Artist at Cannes" drawings on page 5).

Before Caldecott settled in London in the early 1870s to study art seriously, he worked as a banker in Shropshire; hence his knowledge of rural settings and his love for illustrations of the "ye olde" persuasion. He died at the age of forty shortly after arriving in St. Augustine, Florida, on yet another journey in search of scenery and health.

"Caran d'Ache" [Emmanuel Poiré; 1858/9–1909; page 7]. The pseudonym of this famous Paris-based artist is the Russian word for pencil. Born in Moscow as the grandson of a Napoleonic invader, Poiré came to Paris at about age twenty. The five years he spent in the French army made him a specialist at illustrating military subjects (as, for example, in his shadow plays on the Napoleonic era at the artistic cabaret Le Chat

Noir); but his mordant wit and incredibly agile pen were active on all subjects of current interest in numberless Parisian journals. In the 1890s he also contributed to the London humor magazine *Pick-Me-Up* and had this one page in *Punch* (a lampoon on Paderewski). This page was probably the cause for the complaint by the surly American expatriate Joseph Pennell in 1895 that *Punch* was lowering its standards by admitting foreigners.

Poiré had no formal training as an artist, but taught himself by close study of Wilhelm Busch and Adolf Oberländer's contributions to the great Munich humor magazine *Fliegende Blätter*. Like Oberländer, Poiré became a precursor of the comic strip in his subdivided sequential drawings.

"Cham" [Count Amédée de Noé; 1818–1879; page 8]. "Cham" was another highly distinguished French humorous draftsman who merely made guest appearances in *Punch*. The artist's aristocratic family name is the French form of Noah, so for his pseudonym he chose the French form of Ham, son of Noah (pronounced "kam"). Although he worked for several Parisian magazines, his chief loyalty was to the great editor Charles Philipon's *Charivari* (a chief inspiration for *Punch*), on which "Cham" worked for thirty-six years, from 1843 until his death. (After other, loftier career ideas fell through, the young nobleman had been allowed to follow his bent and study art with the eminent painter and lithographer Nicolas Charlet.)

"Cham" visited England in 1842 and thereafter, and was on friendly terms with the *Punch* people (he also contributed work to *The Illustrated London News* and *The Man in the Moon*). He is said to have refused a large sum to start a London humor magazine that would rival *Punch*. For a few months in the heady revolution year of 1848, "Cham" was sole illustrator of a highly liberal journal back home which he proudly called *Punch à Paris*. In the 1859 *Punch* contributions reproduced here, he pokes gentle fun at the adventures of French colonial troopers in the metropolis.

Reginald Cleaver [active 1880s & 1890s; page 9]. Like Boyd, Cleaver (whose less gifted brother Ralph was also working for *Punch* at the same time) represents the highly competent, journalistically trained draftsmen of the 1890s. Before joining *Punch* late in 1891, he had been a chief factor in the success of *The Daily Graphic*, for which he had done Parliamentary reportage. A truly professional artist-for-reproduction, he worked in clean, sharp lines that, among other qualities, were excellent for rendering photographs in the news media of the day. Pennell, not lavish with his praise, and no friend of mass-market zincography, nevertheless stated: "Reginald Cleaver can probably produce a drawing for a cheap process with more success than anyone, and yet, at the same time, his work is full of character." Cleaver also illustrated current fiction.

Alfred Chantrey Corbould [b. 1853, active 1870s–1890s; pages 10–12]. Corbould was a nephew of Charles Keene, who brought him to *Punch* in 1871.

Although he did many kinds of drawings for *Punch* (including the series of "Puzzles" that commented wryly on various inconveniences of London), Corbould was chiefly a humorous illustrator of foxhunts, steeplechases, Rotten Row riders and the like, succeeding Leech and Georgina Bowers as equine artist (indispensable to the magazine, which sold so well among the "horsey" set). Never admitted to the regular Staff of *Punch*, Corbould also worked (at least in the 1890s) for *The Graphic*, *The Daily Graphic*, *The St. James's Budget*, *Black and White*, *St. Paul's* and *The New Budget*. He was a member of the Royal Academy and the Society of British Artists, and his humorous drawings were exhibited in galleries.

"Alfred Crowquill" [Alfred Henry Forrester; 1804–1872; page 13]. On *Punch* in its infancy (he left in 1844), "Crowquill" represents the humorous draftsmanship of the earlier nineteenth century in England, when grotesquerie reigned and academic accuracy of rendering was not a paramount consideration. In the 1820s he produced broadside caricatures and illustrated such writings by his brother Charles Robert Forrester as *Absurdities* ("Alfred Crowquill" was a joint pseudonym of the brothers until Alfred Henry adapted it for himself alone in 1843). A self-taught artist (he was a banker until 1839), "Crowquill" produced a large number of books, many of the texts written by himself, from the 1830s to the 1870s. Among his titles were the *Comic Arithmetic* of 1844 and the *Picture Fables* of 1854; some of his early work was gathered into the album *Phantasmagoria of Fun*. In addition to *Punch*, he worked for *Bentley's Miscellany*. He was remembered as a clever and genial man.

Richard ("Dicky") Doyle [1824–1883; pages 14 & 15]. Doyle had many of the gifts of a truly fine artist; the chief one lacking was the ability to draw. His father, the prominent political cartoonist John Doyle, trained him by a defective method (forbidding the use of models, for instance) that kept Richard virtually an amateur, seemingly incapable of artistic growth, for his entire career. Thus, his best contributions to *Punch* are his tiny vignettes and the wonderful series of "Ye Englyshe in 1849," each plate of which really consists of numerous vignettes massed into a crowd scene. Doyle's longest-lasting contribution to the magazine, of course, was his famous cover design of 1844 (modified 1849), *Punch's* sixth and definitive one—until its covers began to show alterations by 1950 and to change weekly in 1956.

Doyle's kindly wit, whimsy and charm—which remain just as effective today—carried him through. He had work published by the time he was fifteen, and was already famous the next year. Joining *Punch* in 1843, he left it precipitously in 1850 (Tenniel hesitantly replacing him) in protest against a virulent anti-Catholic campaign conducted by the magazine (Doyle was an observant Catholic of Irish ancestry, though born in London). In the 1850s he devoted his time chiefly to book illustration, notable work including his pictures for Ruskin's *King of the Golden River* and Thackeray's *Newcomes*. In 1854 Doyle brought out his own *Foreign Tour of Brown, Jones, and Robinson,* charming picture stories of Englishmen abroad (a few episodes had appeared in *Punch*). In the early 1860s he returned for a while to periodical work, contributing to *The Cornhill Magazine* with such series as "Bird's-Eye Views of Society." In the late 1860s and 1870s he turned increasingly to watercolor, peopling landscapes with captivating elves and sprites. Some of his elfin lore was enshrined in his very popular 1870 color book *In Fairy Land*, now a Victorian classic.

Other important relatives of Richard Doyle were his brother Henry, who became director of the National Gallery of Ireland, and his nephew Arthur Conan Doyle, the physician who created Sherlock Holmes.

George Louis Palmella Busson du Maurier [1834–1896; frontispiece and pages 16–41]. Associated with *Punch* for over thirty years, and one of its true shaping forces, George du Maurier was also its most complex personality in the nineteenth century. Though largely remembered for his polite portrayal of smug upper-class inanities—with an eye to changing fashions in clothing and amusements—his odd bilingual upbringing, his delusions and disappointments, together with a hauntingly accurate memory, led him to utilize his subconscious existence in his art and his novels to an extent not yet customary in his time.

Born in Paris to a French father and English mother (and always believing, wrongly, that the du Mauriers were sunken nobility), young George moved frequently from one Continental city to another. His first long English sojourn was in 1851–56, when he studied chemistry. Turning his thoughts to art, he then studied that subject in Paris (for less than a year), moving to Antwerp in 1857. While there, he suddenly lost the sight of his left eye (probably a detached retina) and sadly gave up his ambition to become a serious painter. While convalescing, he saw the *Punch* Almanack for 1858, admired Leech and began to consider the—somewhat galling—possibility of becoming a mere illustrator.

Returning to England permanently in 1860, du Maurier started contributing not only to *Punch*, but also to *Once a Week*, *The Cornhill Magazine* and *London Society*. His story illustrations in those other journals were more highly finished and painterly than most of his later work; with them he claimed a leading position in the well-known renaissance of English draftsmanship in the 1860s. Even if his *Punch* material was in a lighter vein, there too he and other colleagues began to introduce grace and elegance in place of the cruder bizarreries of the 1840s and 1850s. Du Maurier finally achieved economic security and a lasting artistic home when he succeeded Leech on the regular staff of *Punch* in 1864, furnishing a "romantic tenor" to supplement Keene's "comic bass."

Du Maurier prepared his *Punch* drawings very carefully and professionally so that the wood engraver did not have to "interpret" his lines for the graphic medium, although his crosshatching gave the engraver plenty of work. For years the artist drew directly on the wood block; from 1872, when his other eye became much worse, on paper. (It is said that he henceforth habitually drew on a much larger scale for subsequent photographic reduction, but some extant pen drawings are not appreciably larger than the printed ver-

sions.) A gifted writer, he naturally composed his own captions, which—though now often considered overlong and cumbersome—were then justly admired for their "philological" alertness to many different speech patterns.

Modern critics concur in finding a general decline in du Maurier's skills and standards as time went on, charging him with monotony and shameful facility and usually linking this decline to failing eyesight; only sporadically, they say—as during the Aesthetic craze of the 1870s and early 1880s—was he sufficiently stimulated to create finer drawings. This verdict is somewhat exaggerated and unfair, but it is true that du Maurier privately felt that on *Punch* he (like the mythical house of du Maurier) had come down in the world. (A further disappointment was his failure to inherit the editorship of the magazine after the death of Tom Taylor in 1880.)

Du Maurier still occasionally drew for other publications. In the 1890s, for example, his work appeared in *Black and White* and *The English Illustrated Magazine*. A particularly fruitful association was the one with the American *Harper's Monthly* in the 1880s and 1890s. It was in *Harper's* that his two greatest novels were serialized with his illustrations: *Peter Ibbetson* in 1891 and *Trilby* in 1894.

The du Maurier *Punch* drawings in the present volume, ranging from his "tightest" style in 1861 to his "loosest" in 1893, typify many aspects—not all generally known—of his production: his use of nightmare imagery and the macabre, his Barrie-like fantasy, his striking use of shadows and atmospheric effects, his employment of children's bright sayings, his reportage of London's deprived classes as well as its financially well-off, the use as characters of his own family and pets (including Chang, the Saint Bernard), his wittily prophetic views of the phonograph and television, and his predilection for running series of drawings, such as "Feline Amenities" and "Things One Would Rather Have Left Unsaid."

George was the founder of the real greatness of the du Mauriers, which continued into the present century with his sons Guy, soldier and playwright, and Gerald, superb actor of the 1910s and 1920s, and with Gerald's daughter Daphne, biographer of her gifted clan and author of the immortal *Rebecca*.

Harry Furniss [1854–1925; pages 42–46]. One of the busiest and most characteristic English draftsmen at the turn of the century, Furniss was born in Wexford, Ireland, where his father, an Englishman, was employed as a civil engineer. The family moved to Dublin in 1864. The self-taught young artist produced a journal he dubbed *The Schoolboy's Punch*, and at age seventeen was contributing to *Zozimus*, the Dublin counterpart of *Punch* founded in 1869. Furniss reached London in 1873; three years later he was doing reportorial drawings for *The Illustrated London News*. His first work for *Punch* was in 1880; he joined the *Punch* Table in 1884 (but was always paid by the piece and not salaried) and left the magazine ten years later. In that time span, Furniss estimated, he had supplied over 2600 drawings, always punctually and always in perfect and amicable fulfillment of his assigned task. His *Punch* specialty was Parliamentary reportage, and he was famous for his ability to stalk his quarry stealthily and then bag it (with the pencil) rapidly and accurately. The items reproduced here include an admirable pair of renderings of the House of Commons, as well as an item from his 1888 series depicting English customs in the form of the then rapidly popular Japanese woodcuts. The signature on this series, "Lika Joko," was suggested by *Punch* editor Francis Cowley Burnand.

When Furniss left *Punch* rather angrily, it was chiefly to found his own magazine, which he called— *Lika Joko*. This was soon merged with *The New Budget*, which itself did not outlive 1895. Furniss later did Parliamentary drawings for *The Daily News*. Other publications that printed his work in the 1890s included *The Pall Mall Budget, The St. James's Budget, Black and White, The Sketch, Good Words, Cassell's Family Magazine, The English Illustrated Magazine, The Windsor Magazine* and *Pearson's Magazine*. In 1910 Furniss illustrated the works of Dickens, in 1911 those of Thackeray, but his most famous book commission was for Lewis Carroll's *Sylvie and Bruno* (1889). Furniss wrote a long and tedious autobiography, *The Confessions of a Caricaturist* (1901), as well as fiction. In 1912 he became a writer, actor and director for Edison films in London.

Ernest Henry Griset [1844–1907; page 47]. One of the curious minor talents of the mid-nineteenth century, a humorous *animalier* of more ideas than ability, Griset was born in Boulogne, France, and came to England in the early 1860s. Before long he was doing book illustrations for the Dalziel Brothers (including *Griset's Grotesques*) and for Cassell and Co. (including *Aesop's Fables*). In his brief connection with *Punch*, he was much better on tiny vignettes than on larger drawings. His work also appeared in *Fun, The Graphic* and *Hood's Comic Annual*. In addition, he did pictorial reportage for the American *Harper's Weekly*.

Dudley Hardy [1866/7–1922; page 48]. Hardy and *Punch* come together only at the very end of the era under consideration. Born in Sheffield, Yorkshire, the artist first studied with his father, the marine painter Thomas Bush Hardy, then left for Europe at fifteen and studied at Düsseldorf, Antwerp and Paris. His connection with London magazines began in 1886, and by the end of the century he had contributed to at least twenty of them. At the same time he not only continued to paint all kinds of genre and travel subjects and landscapes, but also became a mighty force in commercial art (influenced by the Frenchmen Jules Chéret and Adolphe Willette), producing magazine ads and some of the famous English posters of the 1890s "golden age" (*A Gaiety Girl, The Chieftain* and others).

Charles Samuel Keene [1823–1891; pages 49–67]. Keene was considered in his day, and has often been since, as occupying the very apex of English pen draftsmanship. Nineteenth-century *Punch* is unthink-

able without him. As scientifically strong as his composition was, however increasingly economical and brilliant his stroke, the general public could always enjoy him as much as the connoisseurs, since they could identify with his comfortable, everyday scenes of the middle class, expressed in a manner that approaches the twentieth-century cartoon in drasticness of gesture and facial expression.

Born in the London area, son of a lawyer, Keene spent some of his childhood among his mother's bourgeois clan in Ipswich. As a youth he studied architecture, then worked for the Whymper family of wood engravers. He began contributing to *The Illustrated London News* in 1847. In the late 1850s and after, he drew for *Once a Week, The Cornhill Magazine* and others, and did book illustration, but his placid bachelor existence was chiefly devoted to *Punch*. His first *Punch* drawing appeared late in 1851; the first one with the famous "CK" signature, in 1854. He was invited to the select *Punch* Table in 1860, but even as a Staff member he preferred to remain unsalaried and thus not constrained to submit work on a regularly recurring basis. Nevertheless, between 1851 and 1890, he contributed between 5000 and 6000 drawings to *Punch*. In 1881 many of his *Punch* pieces were gathered into the volume *Our People*.

Although a scrupulous worker from models and actual locales, Keene almost never created the idea for a drawing, but received suggestions and finished captions from a vast array of friends and colleagues— many, as the captions show, from Scotland and the border counties. For thirty years, for instance, Keene accepted ideas from the ingenious Joseph Crawhall of Newcastle. Sometimes Keene's drawings are merely almost superfluous illustrations of purely verbal gags. Keene is said to have been one of the artists who suffered most from the *Punch* wood engravers' renderings of his subtle originals, but biographers have laid the blame squarely on his shoulders, explaining that what he submitted was not readily suitable for engraving: Keene delighted in pale homemade inks, special pen-points and a variety of washes!

In the twentieth century, one of Keene's best-hidden secrets was posthumously revealed: he had done numerous serious etchings of figures and landscapes.

The artist depicted in the lower drawing on page 49 is a self-portrait.

John Leech [1817–1864; pages 68–81]. One of the best-loved nineteenth-century illustrators in general, Leech was *Punch's* first pictorial potentate. John Flaxman is said to have admired his early, childish efforts in the London coffeehouse owned by Leech's father. The failure of the family business forced Leech to earn a living in other ways, so he turned his artistic bent to profitable ends. Percival Leigh, a fellow student at the medical school Leech was already attending, wrote a *Comic Latin Grammar* that Leech illustrated (Leech's first book work dates from 1835). When Leigh joined the fledgling *Punch*, he brought Leech along. Leech's first drawing for the magazine appeared in its fourth number (1841). Before the artist died in 1864, he had contributed over 3000 items, of which some 600 were "cartoons," that is, the full-page, official "lead" drawings of the week, usually on important political topics.

The other *Punch* items by Leech were smaller "social pictures" on any and all subjects; in this area, Leech was the magazine's first specialist in the "horsey" drawings that celebrated hunting and other types of horsemanship. The artist was himself a passionate hunter, and refused to work more than two figures into his big "cartoons" during the hunting season.

For his *Punch* drawings Leech used no models. He wrote his own captions and made up most of the ideas himself, though in the 1840s Douglas Jerrold, Henry Mayhew, Mark Lemon and other *Punch* writers helped him with the "cartoon" ideas. In the "social pictures," Leech exploited many of his own foibles, manias and pet peeves. Leech's typical sweet, pretty girl was modeled on his own wife, who is said to have been as brainless as she was attractive and to have thoughtlessly aggravated the artist's financial worries — partly caused by a conspicuous parade of gentility that psychologically cloaked his anguish over his father's failure.

Four albums of Leech's *Punch* pieces appeared with the general title *Pictures of Life and Character*. His work for the magazine varied enormously in inspiration and in care of preparation (not until the 1860s were there more stringent standards at *Punch*). Leech is said to have been a prime martyr of the wood engravers, and it is certainly true that his etched and steel-engraved work in many famous book publications (such as the 1844 *Christmas Carol*) looks much finer (especially when aided by cheerful color, as it often was in such cases). Nevertheless, there is some really well-drawn work in *Punch*, and in the 1860s a new bold and broad stroke prepares the way for Keene.

In the present selection, the drawing on page 68 is from the same group of valentines as the one by Browne on page 4; the one on page 81 is from a running series on the feckless sportsman Mr. Briggs; and the one on page 73 — Leech's most famous serious *Punch* "cartoon" — refers to the Crimean War and Russia's disappointed dependence on the rigors of her winter to thwart the English and French invaders.

Phil(ip William) May [1864–1903; pages 82–90]. Like Hardy and Raven-Hill, May typified the jaunty new 1890s approach to humorous art (more akin to twentieth-century cartooning than to academic draftsmanship), but no one rivaled him in neatness and economy of line. His sympathy for the lower classes and for a coarser bohemia also struck a newer note. Self-taught, he was apparently influenced by "Caran d'Ache," but once declared: "All I know I got from Sambourne."

May was born near Leeds. His mother's family was connected with the stage and, as an adolescent, he not only drew for local papers but also helped with scene painting and pantomime design, as well as acting a little (his showmanship was revived later in life when he gave lightning-sketch lectures). Coming to London in 1883, he gained attention by caricaturing stage stars and soon got magazine assignments. Largely for reasons of health, he spent most of 1885–88 in Australia, contributing 900 pictures to *The Sydney Bulletin*. He made his way back to London via Rome and Paris. From then on, he worked for numerous

magazines and brought out several books, including *Phil May's Gutter-snipes* (1896), *Phil May's Sketchbook* and *Phil May's ABC* (both 1897) and an irregularly issued series of Winter and Summer Annuals.

His first work in *Punch* dates from 1893; he was admitted to the august Table in 1895. Before his premature death in 1903 — his precarious health having been further undermined by sociable alcoholism and reckless living — he had contributed nearly 500 drawings to the magazine's regular issues and Almanacks.

(Joseph) Kenny Meadows [1790–1874; pages 91 & 92]. Like "Alfred Crowquill," Meadows was an older-generation artist, typical of the more free-and-easy drawing technique of the 1820s and 1830s. He was one of the first English illustrators whose work was reproduced by wood engraving. Born in Cardigan, Wales, the son of a retired naval officer, Meadows was active in London by at least 1823, when he executed the plates for James R. Planché's *King John* volume. During that decade Meadows also worked for *Bell's Life in London*. His name is chiefly associated with *Heads of the People* (1838–40), a set of sketches of Englishmen in typical employments and walks of life (the text, by Douglas Jerrold and others, was written to go with the pictures); this book was the inspiration for the vastly superior *Les Français peints par eux-mêmes*, produced in the early 1840s and itself internationally imitated. From 1839 to 1843 Meadows did illustrations of Shakespeare. Between 1836 and 1872 he produced much other book work.

Like "Crowquill" and Browne, Meadows was on *Punch* in its earliest days and left in 1844. He then worked for its rivals *The Great Gun* and *The Man in the Moon*. He had already been associated with *The Illustrated London News* from its inception in 1842. Of the two *Punch* "cartoons" included here, one refers to the childhood of the Prince of Wales (born November 9, 1841; later Edward VII), the other to England's inhuman Poor Laws: in the poorhouse, infants were separated from their mothers except at nursing time.

John Everett Millais [1829–1896; page 93]. Millais — one of the foremost English nineteenth-century painters and an eminent illustrator — had only two or three drawings in *Punch*. A child prodigy, he entered the Royal Academy schools at age eleven, remaining there seven years. In 1848 he joined Holman Hunt and Dante Gabriel Rossetti in founding the famous Pre-Raphaelite Brotherhood, blending imaginative coloration with a fragile medieval hieraticism. Millais's later work was much more conventional and easily assimilable by the public. Knighted in 1885, he had just succeeded Frederick Leighton as President of the Royal Academy in 1896 when he, too, died.

Millais's first wood-engraved work appeared in 1855, his contributions to *Tennyson's Poems* in 1857. He then became preeminent in the 1860s artistic renaissance, illustrating Thackeray and Trollope and working for such journals as *Once a Week*, *Good Words*, *The Illustrated London News* and *The Cornhill Magazine*. His masterpiece as an illustrator is *The Parables of Our Lord* (1863).

J. Bernard Partridge [1861–1945; pages 94–105]. As son of a professor of anatomy and nephew of John Partridge, portrait painter extraordinary to the Queen, Bernard Partridge was naturally exposed to the rigorous academic training that betrays its presence even in his wittiest and most appealing sketches. Between 1880 and 1884, he did designs for stained glass and other decorative painting, then turned to magazine work (in the 1890s he contributed to at least thirteen journals), combining this activity both with book illustration (starting with Jerome K. Jerome's popular *Stage-land* in 1889, and continuing with several works by the humorist F. Anstey) and with—acting, side by side with Henry Irving and Johnston Forbes-Robertson, under the pseudonym "Bernard Gould."

Partridge was brought to *Punch* in 1891 by du Maurier, who saw his successor in the younger man. A year later Partridge joined the Staff, and continued to do "social" pictures. In 1899, the academician in him leaping to the fore (and remaining there ever after), he started doing political drawings; in 1901 he took over from Sambourne (who was moving upward to replace Tenniel) as "second [political] cartoonist," and was the magazine's principal cartoonist, again succeeding Sambourne, from 1909 until his death in 1945. Partridge was knighted in 1925.

Leonard Raven-Hill [1867–1942; pages 106–111]. "No one," British art historian James Thorpe wrote of Raven-Hill in 1935, "has ever equalled him for versatility, invention, design, humor, variety of method and artistic feeling." Obviously, Raven-Hill's loose, light and scratchy *Punch* drawings of the 1890s do not tell his full story, but they make it abundantly clear that, like May and Hardy, he was sweeping away academic cobwebs.

Born in Bath as son of a legal stationer, Raven-Hill studied art in London (he was a fellow pupil of C. H. Ricketts and Charles Shannon at Lambeth) and in Paris under the noted academician Adolphe Bouguereau. During the 1890s he was connected with several London magazines, sometimes in leading positions. As art editor of *Pick-Me-Up*, he made that journal a commercial success as well as a matchless training ground for new artistic talents. In 1893 he founded *The Butterfly*, an enormous *succès d'estime* as an art magazine, though he was able to bring out only twelve numbers in a twenty-two-month period. His *Unicorn* of 1895 lasted for only three issues.

Raven-Hill began his association with *Punch* at the turn of 1895–96 and became a Staff member in 1901. Several years later he became a suitably dull "second [political] cartoonist." Poster work also claimed Raven-Hill's attention, as did book illustration, including Kipling's *Stalky and Co.* and H. G. Wells's *Kipps*.

The drawings on pages 109 and 107 (bottom) refer, respectively, to the recruiting campaigns and the manpower shortage during the Boer War.

Edward Tennyson Reed [1860–1933; pages 112 & 113]. Reed is a prime example of the hesitant emergence in *Punch* late in the century of what strikes us as modern cartooning, unacademic drawing in which the line quality is as jolly as the conception—far from being slipshod but free of the pinched crampedness of so much conscious drollery in the nineteenth century. Not only was Reed innocent of academic training; he did not draw at all until he was twenty-three.

His father, a naval architect and M.P. for Cardiff, Wales, opened many doors for him. After leaving Harrow in 1879, E. T. Reed was taken along on a trip to Egypt, China and Japan; his father had designed warships for the Mikado. Then, in the 1880s, E. T. became a welcome guest in the House of Commons, gaining invaluable experience for his future career.

Punch editor Burnand eventually discovered his native talent for drawing and brought him to the magazine in 1889; Reed joined the Staff the next year. His most popular contribution in the first five years on *Punch* was the extremely successful running series "Prehistoric Peeps," anachronistic scenes of cavemen and dinosaurs (begun late 1893). Since his dinosaurs were well researched at the Natural History Museum in South Kensington, his prehistoric drawings were adopted as slides in schools; moreover, theatrical skits were based on them and they were widely imitated by other artists for years to come.

By 1894, when Furniss left *Punch*, Reed had become its Parliamentary cartoonist and filled this post until 1912. In the 1890s he also drew for *The Sketch, The English Illustrated Magazine* and *The Idler*. After *Punch* he worked for *The Bystander*. Albums of his work included *Mr. Punch's Prehistoric Peeps* (1896), *Mr. Punch's Animal Land* (1898) and *Tales with a Twist* (1898).

(Edward) Linley Sambourne [1845–1910; pages 114–126]. Very possibly the greatest authentic genius among nineteenth-century *Punch* draftsmen was Sambourne, who, during a long association with the magazine, developed a dazzling technique in many different styles and blossomed out into a fanciful artist of the first magnitude, blending pictorial and decorative features into monumental and unique full-page compositions. It was clearly a matter of the right man in the right place, for the art historian Forrest Reid felt assured that Sambourne would not have enjoyed the same freedom to experiment on any other magazine of the period. This would have been true at least before the late 1880s.

Sambourne's father, a furrier, was born in Easton, Pennsylvania. Young Edward received no art training beyond the level of technical drawing, which he learned while apprenticed to an engineer. His first contribution to *Punch* was in 1867, and he joined the Staff in 1871. By 1895, when he had long been "second cartoonist," he had submitted some 4000 drawings. (Meanwhile, he was working for several other magazines, being in particular demand for covers!) In 1901 he succeeded Tenniel as principal cartoonist, relinquishing his work only late in 1909, when he was in turn succeeded by Partridge. Sambourne also managed to illustrate a number of books, including *The New Sandford and Merton* (1872) and *Water Babies* (1900).

As political cartoonist in an era of change and

upheaval, Sambourne needed to be able to illustrate just about anything. Apart from such tactics as dressing servants in borrowed uniforms and using them as models, he had recourse to a file of some 10,000 photographs, many of which he had taken himself.

Great as he is, it is very difficult to anthologize Sambourne because his week-to-week subject matter was so inherently topical. Even the relatively clear examples chosen here demand a word of explanation. The portraits on pages 114 (top), 122 and 126 (the last-mentioned of extreme brilliance) are, of course, of Gladstone. In the lower picture on page 114, Disraeli is giving the startled British lion a hairdo like his own, making generous use of "Dizzy's Russian Bear's Grease" (England's triumphs in the Middle East were achieved at the Czar's cost). Page 115 is from the period of the 1877–78 Russo-Turkish War; many Englishmen were eager to get into the scramble, and the music-hall singer called The Great McDermott performed a song (used in the illustration) that began: "We don't want to fight but, by Jingo, if we do . . ."—the source of the political term "jingoism." Few of the innumerable calendrical and zodiacal drawings featured in *Punch* Almanacks have the wit and charm of the one on page 121. The remarkable item on page 123 shows that a hundred years ago Russia was already a serious threat to Afghanistan.

John Tenniel [1820–1914; pages 127–132]. Justly immortalized by his illustrations for *Alice's Adventures in Wonderland* (1865) and *Through the Looking-Glass* (1872), Tenniel was best known in his day as the pillar of *Punch* and the paragon of political cartooning, a genre he "ennobled" and codified to a large extent, followed in this by Thomas Nast in America, his own successors on *Punch* and a host of others to the present day.

Of old Huguenot stock, London-born Tenniel was the son of a master of dancing and arms. The future artist lost the use of one eye in a fencing accident. After a brief period at the Royal Academy schools, Tenniel became a painter and illustrator. In 1845 he won a competition for a House of Lords mural (here was a cartoon, in the traditional sense, paving the way for thousands of magazine "cartoons"). It was his *Aesop's Fables* of 1848 that brought him to the attention of *Punch* late in 1850, when Richard Doyle's abrupt resignation caused havoc. Tenniel wondered whether he could succeed on a humor magazine, and others felt that his style was too classical for the purpose. He remained only fifty years. Soon establishing himself as "second cartoonist" (to Leech's first), he began to be represented by weekly "cartoons" in 1862 and finally succeeded Leech in 1864, staying on as principal cartoonist until the issue of January 2, 1901, whereupon he retired. Almost never leaving London, he produced over 2000 drawings for *Punch*. He was knighted in 1893. Other book illustrations included *Lalla Rookh* (1861, his most highly admired work in his lifetime), *The Ingoldsby Legends* (1864) and participation in *Dalziel's Arabian Nights* (1865).

The subjects of Tenniel's *Punch* "cartoons," decided at the weekly Table meetings, were usually invented by various highly skilled political advisers. In his art, Tenniel never used models, but relied on a well-stocked memory. Nevertheless, as time went on, this proved a drawback, and there were frequent complaints that he made his celebrity protagonists much too young-looking for their current age, and that he constantly depicted obsolete models of mechanical contrivances.

In early days he drew his "cartoons" on transfer paper; afterward, directly on the wood blocks. From 1892 on, he drew on whitened cardboard and his work was photographed onto the wood block. But always the master engraver Swain was forced to "interpret" the drawing, which was rendered in a spare, hard pencil line not eminently suitable for engraving.

As in the case of Sambourne, the anthologist is troubled by excessive topicality but, at the same time, there is far less temptation to reprint a large number of Tenniels: with some striking exceptions, they are much too alike, bloodless and wooden, when seen in the aggregate. The examples here include two early calendars from *Punch* Almanacks, one very close in style (but well drawn!) to Richard Doyle, whom Tenniel had just replaced, the other approaching the style of *Alice*; one of Tenniel's particularly successful portrayals of Disraeli, caught here at a highly historic juncture; an example of *Punch's* social consciousness, not always remembered today in the midst of so much other, more complacent material; a humane reminder based on English experiences in the Zulu Wars; and Tenniel's most famous cartoon, "Dropping the Pilot." The idea for this cartoon, which represents the enforced resignation of Bismarck as the Kaiser looks on, was sent by the absent Gilbert à Beckett to the first *Punch* Table gathering attended by E. T. Reed. As first submitted, the drawing included a two-headed eagle motif unsuitable to the Prussian milieu; this was quickly eliminated after a few copies had been run. The original drawing was presented to Bismarck by Lord Rosebery.

Fred Walker [1840–1875; page 133]. A short-lived genius, Walker was one of the luminaries of the 1860s illustration renaissance. A short, frail man (an elder twin), he was the grandson of a prominent portraitist (William Walker) and son of an artistic jeweler. The young man drew from antiques at the British Museum, spent eighteen months in an architect's office, went to the Royal Academy schools and worked for the noted wood engraver Josiah Wood Whymper. The period from late 1859 to early 1865 was his great magazine era, when his serious drawings appeared in *Good Words*, *Once a Week*, *Everybody's Journal*, *Leisure Hours* and *The Cornhill Magazine*. He began painting —influenced by the Pre-Raphaelites, but remaining eclectic—in 1863, turning to this new medium almost exclusively by 1866. In 1871 he produced one of the first important artistic posters in England, his striking black-and-white announcement for a dramatization of Wilkie Collins' *Woman in White*.

Of Walker's two *Punch* contributions, one is cerebral and less distinctive, whereas the one reproduced here—the only of the artist's many caricatures printed within his lifetime—is very lively, having been called forth by personal observation and indignation at the selfish action. The scene is said to represent Maidenhead on the Thames.

GREAT DRAWINGS
AND ILLUSTRATIONS FROM
PUNCH
1841-1901

A RECOMMENDATION.

Mrs. Cogie. "Ay, that's the new Doctor, Mem; an' I'm sure it wad be an awfu' kindness if ye gied him a bit trial. He had a heap o' Patients when he cam' first, but noo they're a' deid."

10–3–96

THE MATERNAL INSTINCT.

The Master. "I'm sayin', Wumman, ha'e ye gotten the Tickets?"
The Mistress. "Tuts, haud your Tongue aboot Tickets. Let me coont the Weans!"

8–29–96

Alexander Stuart Boyd   1

PESSIMISM.

Artist (irritated by the preliminaries of composition and the too close proximity of an uninteresting native). "I THINK YOU NEEDN'T WAIT ANY LONGER. THERE'S REALLY NOTHING TO LOOK AT JUST NOW."

Native. "AY, AN' I DOOT THERE'LL *NEVER* BE MUCKLE TO LOOK AT THERE!"

5–16–96

Fair Cyclist. "CAN YOU DIRECT ME TO HIGHAM UPLEY, PLEASE?"
Rustic. "YOU 'VE ONLY GOT TO FOLLER YER NOSE, MISS ; BUT YOU 'LL FIND IT UP 'ILL WORK !"

5-29-1901

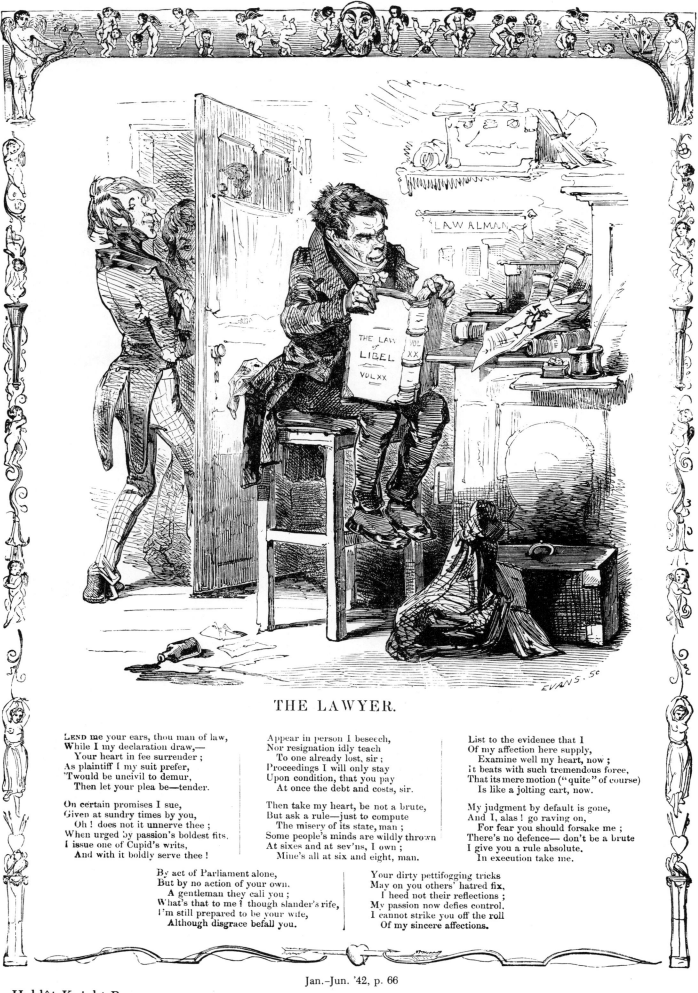

THE LAWYER.

LEND me your ears, thou man of law,
While I my declaration draw,—
    Your heart in fee surrender ;
As plaintiff I my suit prefer,
'Twould be uncivil to demur,
    Then let your plea be—tender.

On certain promises I sue,
Given at sundry times by you,
    Oh ! does not it unnerve thee ;
When urged by passion's boldest fits,
I issue one of Cupid's writs,
    And with it boldly serve thee !

Appear in person I beseech,
Nor resignation idly teach
    To one already lost, sir ;
Proceedings I will only stay
Upon condition, that you pay
    At once the debt and costs, sir.

Then take my heart, be not a brute,
But ask a rule—just to compute
    The misery of its state, man ;
Some people's minds are wildly thrown
At sixes and at sev'ns, I own ;
    Mine's all at six and eight, man.

List to the evidence that I
Of my affection here supply,
    Examine well my heart, now ;
it beats with such tremendous force,
That its mere motion ("quite" of course)
    Is like a jolting cart, now.

My judgment by default is gone,
And I, alas ! go raving on,
    For fear you should forsake me ;
There's no defence— don't be a brute
I give you a rule absolute.
    In execution take me.

By act of Parliament alone,
But by no action of your own.
    A gentleman they call you ;
What's that to me ? though slander's rife,
I'm still prepared to be your wife,
    Although disgrace befall you.

Your dirty pettifogging tricks
May on you others' hatred fix,
    I heed not their reflections ;
My passion now defies control.
I cannot strike you off the roll
    Of my sincere affections.

"WINTER WITH US." (From Our Ironical Artist at Cannes)

Almanack for '79

"WINTER WITH YOU." (From Our Ironical Artist at Cannes.)

Almanack for '79

Randolph Caldecott 5

"WHAT'S IN A NAME?"

Whip. "*WISDOM!* GET AWAY THERE!! *WISDOM!! WISDOM!!!* UGH!—YOU ALWAYS WERE THE BIGGEST FOOL IN THE PACK!"

8–2–79

NOT SUCH DISAGREEABLE WEATHER FOR THE HAYMAKERS
AS SOME PEOPLE THINK.

11–18–82

— „ UNE MÈCHE DE VOS CHEVEUX, MAËSTRO ! "...

MUSICAL COMPETITION.
"A LOCK OF YOUR HAIR, MAËSTRO!"

Almanack for '94

A TURCOS SOLDIER SETTLING WITH A PARISIAN CABMAN.

9–3–59

TURCOS SOLDIER MAKING HIMSELF AT HOME IN A PARISIAN FAMILY.

9–17–59

Chappie (after missing his fourth Stag, explains). "Aw—FACT IS, THE—AW—WAVING GRASS WAS IN MY WAY."
Old Stalker. "HOOT, MON, WAD YE HAE ME BRING OUT A SCYTHE?"

12–5–91

ON THE SANDS AT OSTEND.

Master Tom (knowledge of French—nil). "I SAY, DO I CALL YOU MADAM, OR MADYMOISELLE?"
Mademoiselle. "WHEN ONE DOES NOT KNOW, ONE SAYS MADAME, *N'EST CE PAS*, MONSIEUR?"

8–27–98

PRIVATE VIEW.

Stud Groom (who has looked in). "COMES OF A HARTIS' FAM'LY MYSELF, SIR. MY MOTHER MARRIED AN 'OUSE PAINTER!"

4–23–81

HARDLY NECESSARY.

It flashed across Jones's mind, as his Horse flew over the first Fence, that he really *must* take a few Lessons in Leaping!

12–20–84

Alfred Chantrey Corbould   11

RIVER PUZZLE.

How to get into Molesey Lock?

9–5–85

Old Lady. "Throw that nasty Cigarette away, my good Boy. It makes me quite Ill to see *you* Smoking!"

Boy. "It 'ud make you wuss if yer smoked it yerself, Mum!"

7–23–98

PRIVATE OPINIONS.

GENTS.—"Did you ever see such a rhinoceros?"———RHINOCEROS.—"Vell, I never seed sich monkeys!"

Jan.-Jun. '43, p. 27

AN "AT HOME".   Yᵉ POLKA.

Jan.–Jun. '49, p. 124

"SOCYETYE". ENJOYINGE. ITSELFE. AT·A SOYREÉ.

Jan.–Jun. '49, p. 258

MANNERS. AND. CVSTOMS. OF· Yᵈ ENGLYSHE·IN·1849·   Nº 21.

A. RAYLWAY. STATYON.   SHOWYNGE Yᵉ TRAVELLERS. REFRESHYNGE· THEMSELVES.

Jul.–Dec. '49, p. 52

MR. PEEWIT (goaded into reckless action by the impetuous MRS. P.). *"I—I— I shall report you to your Master, Conductor, for not putting us down at the corner——"*

CONDUCTOR. *"Lor' bless yer 'art, Sir, it ain't my Master as I'm afeard on! I'm like you—it's my MISSUS!"*

10–5–61

Old Mr. Gaffer, disappointed by his model at the eleventh hour, bravely finishes his "Old Applewoman Knitting" from himself—and a Capital piece of Painting it is.

4–11–63

NOVEL ADVERTISING.

OUR FRIEND WITH THE FINE FIGURE HAS ACCEPTED A SUIT OF CLOTHES FROM AN ACCOMMODATING TAILOR. NO MENTION HAS BEEN MADE OF PAYMENT. HE STARS IT ON THE PARADE, AND ENJOYS THE SENSATION HE CREATES, LITTLE KNOWING WHAT USE THE TAILOR'S TOUT IS MAKING OF HIS FASHIONABLE APPEARANCE BEHIND HIS BACK.

Almanack for '65

PHYSICAL STRENGTH v. INTELLECT.

Tom (who has been "shut up" by the Crichton-like accomplishments of his cousin Augustus). "I TAN'T SING, AND I TAN'T 'PEAK FRENSS—BUT I TAN PUNSS YOUR 'ED!"

3-2-67

George du Maurier   17

EVER SINCE POOR JENKINS MET WITH THAT ACCIDENT IN THE HANSOM CAB LAST FORTNIGHT, HIS NOCTURNAL SLUMBERS HAVE BEEN AGITATED BY A CONSTANTLY RECURRING NIGHTMARE. HE DREAMS THAT A MORE THAN USUALLY APPALLING CAB-HORSE BOLTS WITH HIM IN HANWAY PASSAGE (OXFORD STREET); AND CANNOT QUITE MAKE OUT WHETHER HE IS RIDING IN THE CAB, OR WHETHER IT IS HE WHO STANDS, POWERLESS TO MOVE, RIGHT IN FRONT OF THE INFURIATED ANIMAL.

2–15–68

MODEST APPEAL.

Lady (to big drum). "PRAY, MY GOOD MAN, DON'T MAKE THAT HORRID NOISE! I CAN'T HEAR MYSELF SPEAK!"

5–16–68

YOUNG LADIES

WHO AFFECT THE SHORT SKIRT NOW IN VOGUE, ARE RESPECTFULLY CAUTIONED AGAINST THE WITCHING HOUR OF *SUNSET!*

6–13–68

"BY THE SAD SEA WAVES."

Mamma. "SEE, MARION! IN A FEW SECONDS THE SUN WILL SET IN THE OCEAN!"
Marion. "OH, YES, YES! AND *WHAT* A SPLASH THERE WILL BE!"

12–25–69

TALENT APPRECIATED

Jemima Cook. " OH, MARY! HOW *WELL* HE PLAYS!"
Mary Parlourmaid. " DOESN'T HE!! SUCH *EXPRESSION!!!*"

4–24–69

A LITTLE CHRISTMAS DREAM.

Mr. L. Figuier, in the thesis which precedes his interesting work on the World before the Flood, condemns the Practice of awakening the Youthful Mind to Admiration by means of Fables and Fairy Tales, and recommends, in lieu thereof, the Study of the Natural History of the World in which we live. Fired by this Advice, we have tried the Experiment on our Eldest, an imaginative Boy of Six. We have cut off his "Cinderella" and his "Puss in Boots," and introduced him to some of the more peaceful Fauna of the Preadamite World, as they appear Restored in Mr. Figuier's Book.

The poor Boy has not had a decent Night's Rest ever since!

12-26-68

AN INVESTMENT.

"Tell me, my Dear, who's that Little Man they all Seem so dotingly Fond of?"

"*That*, Uncle? Oh, that's Lord Alberic Lackland!"

"Well, he's not much to Look at!"

"No, poor Fellow! But he's awfully Hard Up, and Mamma always Likes to have a Lord at her Dances, so Papa gives him Ten Guineas to Come—that is, *Lends* it, you Know—and a Guinea Extra for every Time my Brother Bob calls him *Ricky!*"

6–25–70

THE MOMENTOUS QUESTION.

Paterfamilias (who is just beginning to feel himself at home in his delightfully new suburban residence) interrupts the Wife of his Bosom.

"'Seaside!' 'Change of Air!!' 'Out of Town!!!' What Nonsense, Anna Maria! Why, good gracious me! what on Earth can you want to be going '*Out of Town*' for, when you've got such a Garden as *this!*"

9–2–71

22   George du Maurier

A COUSINLY HINT.

"How Tall our Shadows are, Claude!" "Yes, aren't they?" "Tall enough for us to be Married, *I* think!"

5-3-73

FROM THE COAL DISTRICTS.

My Lady. "I'm afraid I must give up the Pine-Apple, Mr. Green! Eight Shillings is *really* too much!"
Successful Collier. "Just put 'un up for *me*, then, Master. 'Ere's 'arf a Sovereign; and look 'ere—yer may keep the
Change if yer'll *only tell us* 'ow to Cook 'un!"

10-27-73

ON A BROKEN EGG-SHELL.

Inspired Being. "WHENCE, O WHENCE, LADIES, WHENCE, O WHENCE CAME THE MARVELLOUS INSTINCT THAT PROMPTED THE MINUTE BEING ORIGINALLY CONTAINED IN THIS FRAGILE SHELL TO BURST THE CALCAREOUS ENVELOPE THAT SECLUDED IT FROM THE GLORIES OF THE OUTWARD WORLD?"

Chorus of Admiring Ladies. "WHENCE, O WHENCE, INDEED, MR. HONEYCOMB!"

Master Tommy. "P'RAPS THE LITTLE BEGGAR WAS AFRAID HE'D BE BOILED!"

2–7–74

ART IN EXCELSIS.

THE MONTGOMERY SPIFFINSES HAVE JUST HAD THEIR DRAWING-ROOM CEILING ELABORATELY DECORATED BY ARTISTIC HANDS. THEY ARE MUCH GRATIFIED BY THE SENSATION PRODUCED UPON THEIR FRIENDS.

12–5–74

BAD GRAMMAR, BUT GOOD PLUCK.

"Now, then, Father, just let me *ketch* yer a 'ittin' o' Mother, that's all!"

"I ain't a 'ittin' of her, drat yer!"

"No; but yer was just agoin' to! Let me *ketch* yer, that's all!" [*Seen and heard by y^e Artist.*

7–3–75

A DREAM OF THE SEA.

Ethel, who is not to have a Sea-side Trip this year, Dreams every night that She and her Mamma and Aunt and Sisters spread their Sash-bows and Panniers and Fly away to the Yellow Sands.

9–18–75

George du Maurier   25

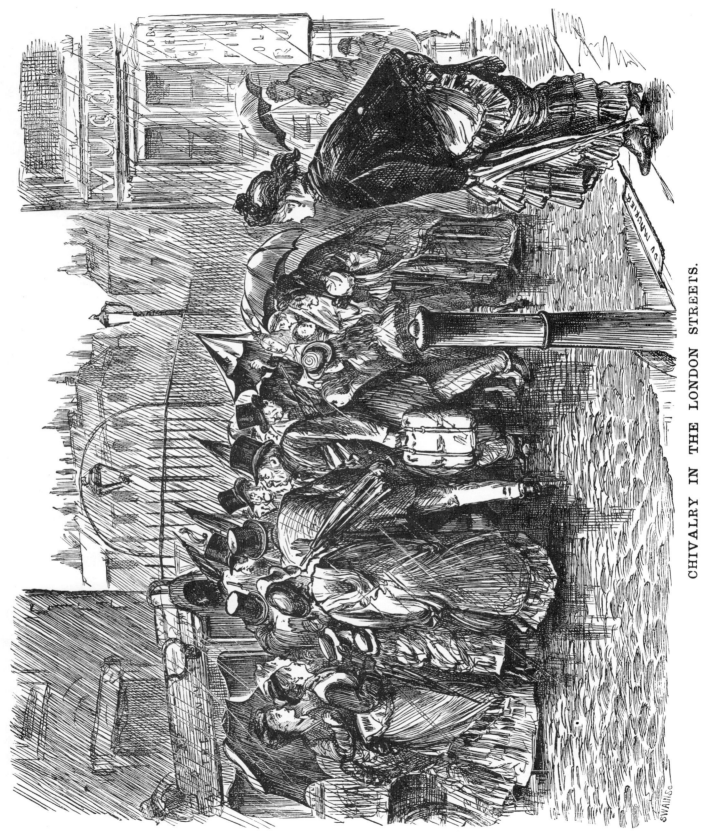

CHIVALRY IN THE LONDON STREETS.

To be observed on a Rainy Day at any Omnibus Station.

Almanack for '76

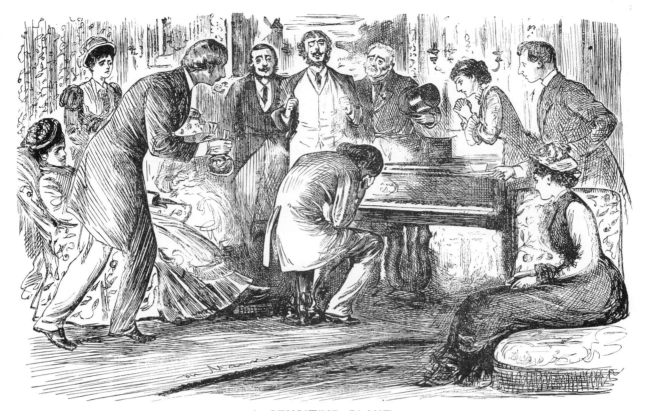

A SENSITIVE PLANT.

(HERR PUMPERNICKEL, HAVING JUST PLAYED A COMPOSITION OF HIS OWN, BURSTS INTO TEARS.)

Chorus of Friends. "OH, *WHAT* IS THE MATTER? WHAT CAN WE DO FOR YOU?"
Herr Pumpernickel. "ACH! NOSSING! NOSSING! BOT VEN I HEAR REALLY *COOT* MUSIC, ZEN MUST I ALWAYS *VEEP!*"

8–11–77

CONFUSION OF CAUSE AND EFFECT.

Maggie. "OH, TOMMY!! LOOK AT THAT *SWEET* LITTLE THING!!! I'M AFRAID IT 'S AFRAID OF *CHIMBORAZO!* JUST WAG *CHIMBO-RAZO'S* TIL, TO PUT HIM IN A GOOD TEMPER, THERE 'S A GOOD BOY!"

11–24–77

George du Maurier 27

BY THE TELEPHONE SOUND IS CONVERTED INTO ELECTRICITY, AND THEN, BY COMPLETING THE CIRCUIT, BACK INTO SOUND AGAIN. JONES CONVERTS ALL THE PRETTY MUSIC HE HEARS DURING THE SEASON INTO ELECTRICITY, BOTTLES IT, AND PUTS IT AWAY INTO BINS FOR HIS WINTER PARTIES. ALL HE HAS TO DO, WHEN HIS GUESTS ARRIVE, IS TO SELECT, UNCORK, AND THEN COMPLETE THE CIRCUIT; AND THERE YOU ARE!

Almanack for '78

EDISON'S TELEPHONOSCOPE (TRANSMITS LIGHT AS WELL AS SOUND).

(*Every evening, before going to bed, Pater- and Materfamilias set up an electric camera-obscura over their bedroom mantel-piece, and gladden their eyes with the sight of their Children at the Antipodes, and converse gaily with them through the wire.*)

Paterfamilias (in Wilton Place). "BEATRICE, COME CLOSER, I WANT TO WHISPER."   *Beatrice (from Ceylon).* "YES, PAPA DEAR."
Paterfamilias. "WHO IS THAT CHARMING YOUNG LADY PLAYING ON CHARLIE'S SIDE?"
Beatrice. "SHE'S JUST COME OVER FROM ENGLAND, PAPA. I'LL INTRODUCE YOU TO HER AS SOON AS THE GAME'S OVER?"

Almanack for '79

MISPLACED CHARITY.

On coming out of Church, General Sir Talbot de la Poer Sangrazul is so struck by the beauty of the Afternoon Sky, that he forgets to put on his Hat, and Lady Jones (who is rather Near-sighted) drops a Penny into it!

3–1–79

THE HEIGHT OF ÆSTHETIC EXCLUSIVENESS.

Mamma. "Who are those extraordinary-looking Children?"
Effie. "The Cimabue Browns, Mamma. They're Æsthetic, you know!"
Mamma. "So I should imagine. Do you know them to speak to?"
Effie. "Oh dear no, Mamma—they're most exclusive. Why, they put out their Tongues at us if we only look at them!"

11–1–79

George du Maurier   29

REFINEMENTS OF MODERN SPEECH.

SCENE—*A Drawing-room in " Passionate Brompton."*

Fair Æsthetic (suddenly, and in deepest tones, to Smith, who has just been introduced to take her in to Dinner). "ARE YOU INTENSE?"

6–14–79

THE MUTUAL ADMIRATIONISTS.

(Fragments overheard by Grigsby and the Colonel at one of Prigsby's Afternoon Teas.)

Young Maudle (to Mrs. Lyon Hunter and her Daughters). "IN THE SUPREMEST POETRY, SHAKSPEARE'S, FOR INSTANCE, OR POSTLETHWAITE'S, OR SHELLEY'S, ONE ALWAYS FEELS THAT, &C., &C., &C."

Young Postlethwaite (to the three Miss Bilderbogies). "THE GREATEST PAINTERS OF ALL, SUCH AS VELASQUEZ, OR MAUDLE, OR EVEN TITIAN, INVARIABLY SUGGEST TO ONE, &C., &C., &C."

5–22–80

A POSER.

"IT'S NOT SO MUCH A *DURABLE* ARTICLE THAT I REQUIRE, MR. CRISPIN. I WANT SOMETHING *DAINTY*, YOU KNOW—SOMETHING *COY*, AND AT THE SAME TIME JUST A WEE BIT *SAUCY!*"

10–30–80

THE SIX-MARK TEA-POT.

Æsthetic Bridegroom. "IT IS QUITE CONSUMMATE, IS IT NOT?"
Intense Bride. "IT IS, INDEED! OH, ALGERNON, LET US LIVE UP TO IT!"

10–30–80

HARE AND HOUNDS—AND MAY THEIR SHADOWS NEVER GROW LESS.

Mrs. Miniver. "HOW EXHAUSTED THEY LOOK, POOR FELLOWS! FANCY DOING THAT SORT OF THING FOR MERE PLEASURE!"

Little Timpkins (his bosom swelling with national pride). "AH, BUT IT'S ALL THROUGH DOING THAT SORT OF THING FOR *MERE PLEASURE*, MIND YOU, THAT WE ENGLISH ARE—*WHAT WE ARE!*" [*Bully for little Timpkins!*

3–5–81

COLONISING IN IOWA, U.S.

(*A Hint to the Younger Sons of our Aristocracy, and eke to the Daughters thereof.*)

Lady Maria. "HOW *LATE* YOU ARE, BOYS! YOUR BATHS ARE READY, AND I'VE MENDED YOUR DRESS TROUSERS, JACK. SO LOOK SHARP AND CLEAN YOURSELVES, AND THEN YOU CAN LAY THE CLOTH, AND KEEP AN EYE ON THE MUTTON WHILE EMILY AND I ARE DRESSING FOR DINNER."

Lord John. "ALL RIGHT. HOW MANY ARE WE TO LAY FOR?"

Lady Emily. "EIGHT. THE TALBOTS ARE COMING, AND MAJOR CECIL IS GOING TO BRING THE DUKE OF STILTON, WHO'S STOPPING WITH HIM."

11–12–81

George du Maurier   33

SEA-SIDE SPORTS.—TOBOGGANING AT WHITBY.

Miss Eva Bedell. "Oh! do *look* at what a lovely game those dear little Boys are playing at, Miss Smart! Mightn't Me and Maud play at it too?"

The New Governess. "Certainly not, Eva. I feel sure Sir Pompey would consider such a proceeding most Unladylike!"

9-16-82

THE FESTIVE SEASON.—A PROUD MOMENT.

1–6–83

MUSIC AT HOME. (THE EGOISM OF GENIUS.)

Eminent Violinist. "Dell me—who is dat liddle pald old Chendleman viz ze vite viskers and ze bince-nez, looking at ze Bigchus?"

Hostess. "It's my Uncle Robertson. I'm grieved to say he is quite Deaf!"

Eminent Violinist. "Ach, I am zo zorry for him! He vill not pe aple to hear me blay ze Vittle!"

8–11–83

George du Maurier   35

THOSE BROWNS AND THEIR LUMINOUS PAINT AGAIN.

10–27–83

IN SLUMMIBUS.

Small Eastendian. "Ello! 'ere's a Masher! Look at 'is Collar an' 'At!"

5–3–84

THINGS ONE WOULD RATHER HAVE LEFT UNSAID.

Scene—*A Concert for the People.*

Distinguished Amateur (about to make his First Appearance in Public). "Oh, I do feel so Nervous!"
Sympathetic Friend. "Oh, there's no occasion to be Nervous, my dear Fellow. They Applaud *anything*!"

1–3–85

ADVERTISING IN EXCELSIS.

Mrs. Blokey, Junior (who is of a romantic turn). "My! ain't the Moon lovely, glitterin' on the Wyves! It does one's Heart good to see it!" *Mr. B. (Blokey and Son).* "Ah! and wouldn't it do one's 'Art good to see 'Blokey and Son's Pickles' printed right across it in Capital Letters, big enough for all the World to read with the Naked Hi!"

Almanack for '86

George du Maurier 37

SIC TRANSIT!

Effie. "Poor things! I suppose they're going to the Funeral of that poor Dead Horse! That's why they look so sad!"

11–23–86

WINDOW STUDIES.—A QUIET PIPE.

(In Remembrance of March, 1887.)

4–2–87

WINDOW STUDIES.
A HARMONY IN LONDON SMUT.
2–16–89

A NEW GAME.
Tommy (to his French Nurse). " PASSEZ, THÉRÈSE ! "
4–13–89

FELINE AMENITIES.

Fair Hostess (who is proud of her popularity). "YES; I FLATTER MYSELF THERE'S NOT A DOOR-BELL IN THE WHOLE STREET THAT'S SO OFTEN RUNG AS MINE!" *Fair Visitor.* "WELL, DEAR, I HAD TO RING IT *FIVE TIMES!*"

7–6–89

WHAT OUR ARTIST (THE ILLUSTRATOR) HAS TO PUT UP WITH.

Fair Authoress. "AND, FOR THE FRONTISPIECE, I WANT YOU TO DRAW THE HEROINE STANDING PROUDLY ERECT BY THE SEA-SHORE, GAZING AT THE STILL IMAGE OF HERSELF IN THE TROUBLED WAVES. THE SUN IS SETTING; IN THE EAST THE NEW MOON IS RISING—A THIN CRESCENT. HER FACE IS THICKLY VEILED; AN UNSHED TEAR IS GLISTENING IN HER BLUE EYE; HER SLENDER, WHITE, JEWELLED HANDS ARE CLENCHED INSIDE HER MUFF. THE CURLEWS ARE CALLING, UNSEEN——"

F. A.'s Husband. "YES; DON'T FORGET THE CURLEWS—THEY COME IN CAPITALLY! I CAN LEND YOU A STUFFED ONE, YOU KNOW —TO DRAW FROM!" &C., &C., &C., &C., &C.

7–19–90

THE OLD COUNTRY. ST. WYCLIFFE'S COLLEGE, OXBRIDGE.

Mr. Jonah P. Skeggs, from Chicago (with his family) suddenly bursts on Jones, who keeps at Letter A in the Cloisters.

"Sir — we offer you — many Apologies — for this — unwarrantable Intrusion ! We were not aware the Old Ruin was Inhabited !"

3-11-93

A LESSON IN ALTRUISM.

Always be kind to Dumb Animals — their Lives are short, and should be made Happy and as Comfortable as possible — even at the cost of a little Temporary Discomfort to yourself.

4-8-93

A QUIET SUNDAY IN LONDON; OR, THE DAY OF REST.

3-20-86

HOW WE ADVERTISE NOW.

12-3-87

Harry Furniss   43

ESSENCE OF PARLIAMENT.
Extracted from the Diary of TOBY, M.P.

House of Commons, Monday, August, 19.—As many pages of this Diary bear record, I have profound respect and admiration for JOSEPH GILLIS. His simplicity of character, his directness of purpose, his genial bearing, his enlightened mind, and his oratorical gifts ever attract me. JOEY B., as was written long ago, is sly—dev'lish sly. No use impecunious member of the community whose financial interests are entrusted to his care coming round him with pleas about drawing a month's, or even a week's, salary in advance. JOSEPH, without causing wing of friendship to moult a feather, ever understands their blandishments. He knows what he's about, and generally accomplishes his end, performing the maximum of public good with the minimum of personal estrangement.

To-day JOSEPH shines in new and brighter light. BALFOUR, desirous of mixing little treacle with the brimstone usually administered to Irish Members, brought in series of Bills appropriating Imperial funds for local works in Ireland. Irish Light Railways Bill one of group. Proposes to advance over half a million sterling towards cost of Irish

8-31-89

THE HOUSE OF COMMONS FROM TOBY'S PRIVATE BOX.

3-29-90

FISHING ROD'RICK DHU ABOUT THIS TIME IN SCOTLAND.

8-25-88

DISSECTING ROOM, ZOOLOGICAL GARDENS.

SCIENTIFIC CELEBRITIES TAKING THE CAST OF A WHALE.

5-25-67

Ernest Griset 47

Sarah (to Sal). "LOR! AIN'T 'E 'ANDY WITH 'IS FEET!"

7–18–1900

48   Dudley Hardy

SMART, FOR THE EASTERN COUNTIES.

Old Lady. " Oh, you bad Boy ! where did you get all that Holly from ! Don't you know your Catechism enjoins you to keep your hands from ' Picking and Stealing ? ' " Boy. " Yes, 'm, and ' yar' tongue from evil Speakin', Lyin', and Slanderin', tew ! "

1–1–59

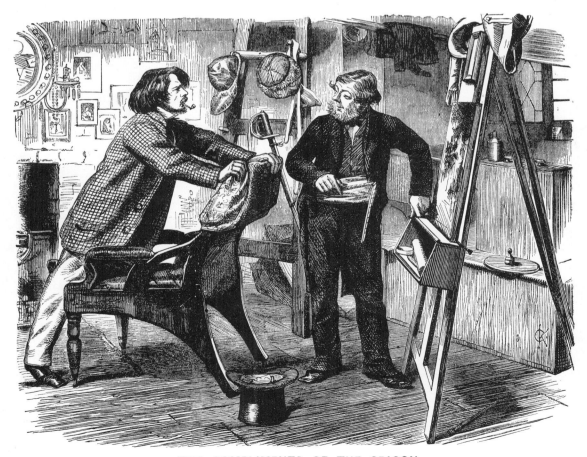

THE COMPLIMENTS OF THE SEASON

Frame-Maker (who comes to measure STODGE's Academy pictures). " Now, I think it's a pity you don't let me have some o' these for my Winder, since you have no idea of the amount of Rubbish I can get rid of at times."

3–12–59

Charles Keene   49

SCIENCE.

Professor Parallax (enthusiastically). "OH! MY DEAR MRS. S., IF YOU CAN MANAGE TO STOOP DOWN, HERE IS 'CAPELLA' SHOWN MOST BEAUTIFULLY!!"
[*But by this time, it being a fine frosty night, poor* MRS. SPUDGROVE, *having seen the Moon, and Jupiter and his Satellites, and Saturn, and Double Stars, and no end of Nebulæ, had had almost enough of it!*

Almanack for '68

"OH, I DARE SAY!"

Helen (19). "OH, I SAY, COUSIN GEORGE, IF IT WASN'T FOR 'MA SITTING THERE, WOULDN'T THIS BE LIKE THAT BEAUTIFUL CAVE IN CHARLES READE'S '*FOUL PLAY*,' WHERE YOU KNOW——"
[*Cousin George (ditto) was just going to say that the same idea had struck him, &c., when 'Ma rose, and called out it was time to go home to tea!*

9–26–68

50   Charles Keene

"FINE ART," 1869.

Rural Connoisseur. "He's a P'intin' Two Pictur's at Once, d' yer See? 'Blest if I don't Like that there Little 'Un as he's got his Thumb through, the Best!"

Almanack for '70

A TARTAR!

"*** In Truth he was a Noble Steed,   Who looked as though the Speed of Thought
A Tartar of the Ukraine Breed,   Were in his Limbs——"
                                          [*Our Animal Painter has to make the best of his Model!*

3–5–70

AT THE BOAT-RACE.

Ada. " MAMMA, I CAN'T QUITE MAKE OUT WHAT THOSE ROUGH-LOOKING MEN ARE SAYING ; BUT THEY MUST BE WELL-EDUCATED ! "
Mamma. " WHY, DEAR ? "
Ada. " WELL, THEY ALL SEEM TO KNOW THE FRENCH FOR ' LADY ' " ! !

3–31–77

NON BEN (LOMOND) TROVATO.

Rory (fresh from the hills). " HECH, MON ! YE 'RE LOASSIN' A' YER WATTER ! ! "
Aungus. " HAUD YER TONGUE, YE FEUL ! ETT 'S LATT OOT TO STOAP THE LADDIES FRAE RIDIN' AHINT ! ! "

10–30–80

SEASONABLE WEATHER, 1881—SO DELIGHTFUL!

Old Gent. "Now, you Boys! I will not have——" (*Snowball!*)

1-29-81

"DISTHRESS!"

Sergeant (to Milkwoman). "You appear to be doing a great deal of Business just now, Mrs. Murphy."
Mrs. Murphy. "Sorra a bit! I'm nearly Kilt wid thryin' to Live!"

7-1-82

Charles Keene   53

AN ULTIMATUM.

Cabby (Master of the Situation). "TAKE UP YOUR MASTER AT CAVEL'SH SQUARE? NOW, LOOK 'ERE, YOUR GOV'NER 'LL HEV TO COME HISSELF,—AND TELL ME WHERE HE WANT TO GO, AN' HE CAN MAKE ME A HOFFER!"

2–5–81

"THE RULE OF THE ROAD."

Both Conductors. "'Ere y' are, Lady!—I ketched 'old of 'er fust!—Just you drop 'er, will yer!—You're a——"
(*Shrieks from Child.*) "I' got the Baby, Mum!"
[*She ultimately became prize to the "Car Company," but, as she complained to the Passengers, with her clothes nearly "tore off her back!"*

8–5–82

ASSURING!

Passenger (faintly). "C'lect Fares—'fore we get across! I thought we——"
Mate. "Beg y'r pardon, Sir, but our Orders is, in Bad Weather, to be partic'lar careful to collect Fares: 'cause in a Gale like this 'ere, there's no knowing how soon we may all go to the Bottom!"

8–11–83

RETROSPECTION.

SCENE—*Æsthetic Neighbourhood.*

Converted Betting Man (plays First Concertina in Salvation Army Band). "POOTY 'OUSES THEY BUILDS IN THESE SUBU'BS, MR. SWAGGET."

Mr. S. (Reformed Burglar and Banner-Bearer in the same). "AH! AND HOW 'ANDY THEM LITTLE BAL-CO-NIES WOULD 'A' BEEN IN FORMER——"

[*A warning flourish on the Concertina, and Mr. S. drops the subject!*

8–25–83

ART IN THE MIDLANDS.

Visitor (at the Shoddyville Art Gallery). "WHO PAINTED THIS PORTRAIT, DO YOU KNOW?"
Curator. "I BELIEVE BY SOME LONDON FIRM, SIR!!"

9–22–83

Charles Keene 57

VOLUNTEER TACTICS AT OUR AUTUMN MANŒUVRES.

Captain Wilkinson (excitedly, to Major Walker, of the Firm of Wilkinson, Walker, & Co , Auctioneers and Estate Agents). "Don't you think we'd better bring our Right Wing round to attack the Enemy's Flank, so as to prevent their occupying those empty Houses we have to let in Barker's Lane?!"

Almanack for '85

"DESIRABLE!"

Saxon Passenger (on Highland Coach). "Of course you're well acquainted with the Country round about here. Do you know 'Glen Accron'?"

Driver. "Aye, weel." *Saxon Passenger (who had just bought the Estate).* "What sort of a Place is it?"

Driver. "Weel, if ye saw the Deil tethered on't, ye'd just say 'Puir Brute'!"

10–24–85

EXPLANATORY.

Old Gent (in agony). "Ph-e-e-w! Conf——I wish you'd Look where you Step, Sir!"
Passenger (leaving—"Chrish'm'sh time—only oncshe 'Year'!). "'Beg tel thousal Pard'l'sh, Shir! 'Diff'cully I fin' 'sh t' Shtep where I Look!!"

1–16–86

LEGISLATION.

Alderman Gustle, M.P. (reading Paper at his mid-day snack). "Oh, I dessay! Go down to the 'Ouse at Two o'Clock, indeed! Why, it wouldn't give me no time for Luncheon! Oh, I shall Vote against that!"

3–13–86

Charles Keene   59

STARTLING !

Constable (to Nervous Passenger, arrived by the Ramsgate Train). "I 'VE GOT YER"—("*Ger-acious Heavens !*" *thinks little Skeery with a thrill of horror.* "'*Takes me for somebody that 's 'wanted' !*'")—"A CAB, SIR '"

5–29–86

"THE OLD ADAM."

The Minister (coming on them unawares). "E-E-H ! SANDY MCDOUGAL ! AH 'M SORRY TO SEE THIS ! AND YOU TOO, WULLY ! FISHIN' O' THE SAWBATH ! AH THOUCHT AH 'D ENSTELLET BETTER PRENCIPLES——" (*A Rise.*) "E-E-EH ! WULLY, MAN !—YE HAE 'M !—IT 'S ENTIL 'M ! HAUD UP YER R-ROD, MAN—OR YE 'LL LOSE 'M—TAK' CAR-R-RE !——" [*Recollects himself, and walks off.*

12–4–86

Keeper (to the two Tourists, who find Canoeing more difficult on the Highland Rivers than on the Thames). "HI! HOY! HOY! D' YE NO KEN THIS IS THE MCCHIZZLEM'S PRIVATE WATTER!?"

Almanack for '87

OUR CHRISTMAS CONCERT.

The Rector (who conducts the Rehearsal). "SUPPOSE WE TRY THAT MOVEMENT AGAIN? I THINK, MR. FOOTLES, YOU WERE HALF A BAR BEHIND IN TAKING UP YOUR POINT. OH DEAR!—YOU 'RE NOT GOING, MR. FOO——"
Mr. Footles (our Flauto Secondo, huffed). "YESSIR. 'F YOU 'RE SO PERTIC'LAR 'S T'ALF A BAR, I SHA'N'T JINE THE S'CIETY!!"

1-8-87

THE FORCE OF HABIT.

Our County Member (attending Church during the Recess). "I BEG TO MOVE, SIR, THAT THE
QUESTION BE NOW PUT!"

6–4–87

JUBILEE TIME.

Sweeper (surprised at receiving a Shilling). "'THANK YER 'ONOUR, AN' MAY THE BLISSED
SAINTS PAY YER BACK A THOUSAND THOIMES!"
City Crœsus (having "done the sum"). "PHOOUGH! ON'Y FIFTY POUNDS!"

6–25–87

Charles Keene 63

PREDESTINED!

Northern Matron (before the School-Board). "I'M NOT AGAINST EDDICATION, LADIES AND GEN'L'MEN. I AL'AYS MAKE HIM TAKE HIS BOOK O' NIGHTS. BUT REELLY I CALLS IT A FLYIN' IN THE FACE O' PROVIDENCE TO BE KEEPIN' A BOY OUT O' THE STABLES WITH SUCH A PAIR O' LEGS AS HIS'N!!"

2-26-87

"ICHABOD!"

Scotch Wife (to her Gossip). "AH DINNA KEN WHAT'S COME OWER THE KIRK. AH CANNA BIDE TO SEE OOR MENESTER SPANKIN' ABOOT ON YON CYCLOPÆDY!"

10-8-87

"RETRENCHMENT."

First Coster (in Trap). "WE SHALL SEE YOU AN' THE MISSUS AT EPSOM AS USUAL, BILL?"

Second Ditto. "NO; THE TIMES AIN'T PERPITIOUS, 'ARRY." (*Shaking his head.*) "NO. WI' GOSCHEN A REDOOCIN' THE OLD WOMAN'S MARRIAGE SETTLEMENT, AND BIT O' MONEY IN CONSOLS, AN THE EXTRYS ON CHAMPAGNE,—NOT TO SAY AS THE MOKE MIGHT ARTERWARDS BE CHARGED AS A PLEASURE-'ORSE,—AN' THE WHEEL-TAX, AN' ONE THING AN' ANOTHER—IT DON'T RUN TO IT, MY BOY!!" [*Retires ruefully.*

5-26-88

RESIGNATION.

Sympathetic Old Gentleman. "I'M SORRY TO SEE YOUR HUSBAND SUFFER SO, MA'AM. HE SEEMS VERY——"

Lady Passenger (faintly). "OH DEAR! HE ISN'T MY HUSBAND. 'SURE I DON'T KNOW WHO THE GE'TLEMAN IS!"

Almanack for '89

"IN TERROREM."

Street Boy (to Old Lady). "THE BOARD O' WORKS IS A COMIN' UP THE NEX' STREET, AN'
IF THEY SEES YOUR DOOR AIN'T SWEP'—YOU'LL KETCH IT!"

Almanack for '89

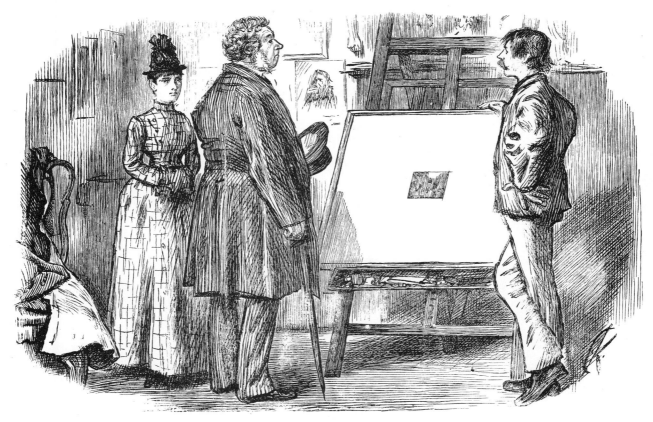

PROPORTIONS.

Buyer. "In future, as my Collection increases, and my Wall-space is limited, and Price no object, perhaps you would let me have a little more 'Picture,' and a little less 'Mount'!"

5-11-89

THE CHEAP FARES.

Passengers. "We're Full—there's no room!"
Conductor. "We must make Room for 'er. There's Room for One on the Near Side 'ere. B'sides you're all short Penn'orths, and she's a Fourpenn'orth—goes the whole way!"

5-3-90

Charles Keene   67

THE PET PARSON.

OH, darling of spinsters !—who, casting away
    The earth and its follies, its pomps and its pother,
With footman behind them ride meekly to pray,
    And lose this vain world in the joys of another !—
'Tis sweet in the pulpit to see how thou'lt stand,
    All scented and curl'd before Heaven's high throne,—
To mark the soft wave of thy diamond-deck'd hand,
    Th' odour of sanctity—*eau de Cologne !*

How cautiously, gingerly, lisp'st thou of death,—
    With soft, under-tones dost thou *coo* about hell !—
The grim King of Terrors is—shortness of breath ;
    Perdition—a place where the vulgarest dwell !
And, tender physician of luxury's souls !—
    When made to prescribe for their filthiest taints,
If brimstone thou *must* put in naughty men's bowls,
    'Tis brimstone with treacle—a med'cine for saints

And how **art** thou welcomed to revel and rout,
    Where claret runs brightly as martyrdom's blood !
An orthodox spell to keep naughtiness out,
    An elegant piece of the pious and good !
When wealth—as wealth must—walk in wickedness' ways,
    And take the bad breath of the pestilent hag,—
If straying with thee, wealth is safe as she strays,—
    As babies midst fevers, with camphor in bag !

Thou dear Valentine to the " mis'rable " crew,—
    The " sinners " in purple and cambric attire,--
Who shudder at death—in the family pew,
    And think—once a week upon Sathanas' fire !—
Still make Heaven easy to those who have gold,
    To be sought without doubtings, or faintings, or cares,
Not e'en by the ladder the Jew saw of old,
    But up a broad flight of soft carpeted stairs !

THE CHARITY BALL.

Having purchased a ticket for a Charity Ball, you are deluded by the promise of a pretty Partner to waltz, and are victimized as above.

Jan.–Jun. '43, p. 87

THE MAYORALTY.—THE COMING IN.

Jul.–Dec. '44, p. 208

THE MAYORALTY.--THE GOING OUT.

Jul.-Dec. '44, p. 209

THE GAME LAWS;

OR, THE SACRIFICE OF THE PEASANT TO THE HARE.

Jul.–Dec. '44, p. 197

'GENERAL FÉVRIER" TURNED TRAITOR.

"Russia has Two Generals in whom she can confide—Generals Janvier and Février."—*Speech of the late Emperor of Russia.*

Jan.-Jun. '55, p. 95

BLOOMERISM—AN AMERICAN CUSTOM.

Jul.–Dec. '51, p. 141

IMITATION.

Master Jackey having seen a "Professor" of Posturing, has a private performance of his own in the Nursery.

Jul.–Dec. '48, p. 130

THE TOO FAITHFUL TALBOTYPE.

Georgina (in riding habit). "Well dear! I declare it's the very image of you! I never!"

Sarah Jane (who insists upon seeing the plate). "Like me! For goodness sake don't be ridiculous, Georgina. I think it's Perfectly Absurd! Why, it has given me a stupid little Turn-up Nose, and a Mouth that's absolutely Enormous!"

Jan.–Jun. '55, p. 256

John Leech   75

A NICE BRACING DAY AT THE SEA-SIDE.

Almanack for '56

PROPRIETY IN DRESS.

SHORT dresses have been objected to by the prudish ; but though the clothes of ladies are now more than long enough, they admit of the very greatest latitude. — N.B. The discovery of the latitude has succeeded that of the longitude.

NATIONAL HUMILIATION.—Monday, the 22nd of June, is the anniversary of the imposition of the Income-Tax. Persons in the receipt, or no longer in the receipt of precarious incomes, fast.

WHY is a youth like a Church robbed of its bibles and prayer-books, &c ?— He is in a state of pew-pillage.

PHILOSOPHY FOR THE TURF.—He who lays wagers, lays golden eggs. The goose did so: and you know the consequence.

TAXIDERMY FOR PARENTS. — If you want to preserve your children, do not stuff them.

A CAVALIER.

Adolphus. " NOW, GIRLS!—IF YOU'RE GAME FOR A RIDE ON THE SANDS—I'M YOUR MAN

Almanack for '57

SINGULAR DELUSION.

A popular preacher received so many pairs of slippers from the female part of his congregation, that he got to fancy himself a centipede.

WAR AND CIVILISATION. — A file of British soldiers is generally found to polish a barbarous enemy

OBLIGED TO CUT HIS STICK.—When a man draws upon the bank of nature, he first sends in the woodmen with their bills.

DOMESTIC MORAL. —Those Mammas must regard their daughters as mere dirt who are desirous of getting them off their hands.

THE CONSERVATIVE CLUB.—The emblem of this orderly association is the policeman's bludgeon.

THE HANDS.—It is quite an error to suppose that filbert nails are more liable to crack than others.

A GLUTTON'S VIRTUE.—Resignation to his *fête*.

THANK GOODNESS! FLY-FISHING HAS BEGUN!

Miller. "Don't they, really! Perhaps they'll rise better towards the cool of the Evening, they mostly do!"

4–25–57

A WHOLESOME CONCLUSION.

Lady Crinoline. "Yes, Love—a very Pretty Church, but the Door is certainly very Narrow!"

2-6-58

PHOTOGRAPHIC BEAUTIES.

"I say, Mister, Here's me and my mate wants our Fotergruffs took; and mind, we wants 'em 'Ansom, cos they're to give to two Ladies."

6-19-58

HUSBAND-TAMING.

Almanack for '59

SCENE IN A TUNNEL. HOW TO CLEAR A CARRIAGE FOR A CIGAR.

Ferocious Looking Passenger (to Old Gent who objects to Smoking). "That's a Pretty Knife; ain't it? That's the sort o' thing we use in California! Jolly thing to Stick into a Fellow, Eh?"

[Old Gent *fears his Companion is not "quite right," and changes his Carriage at the next Station.*

1-9-64

THE DEER ARE DRIVEN FOR MR. BRIGGS. HE HAS AN EXCELLENT PLACE, BUT WHAT WITH WAITING BY HIMSELF SO LONG, THE MURMUR OF THE STREAM, THE BEAUTY OF THE SCENE, AND THE NOVELTY OF THE SITUATION, HE FALLS ASLEEP, AND WHILE HE TAKES HIS FORTY WINKS, THE DEER PASS!

Almanack for '61

John Leech   81

FOGGY WEATHER.

"Has Mr. Smith been here?"   "Yes; he was here about an Hour ago."
"Was I with him?"

3–3–94

Q. E. D.

"WHAT'S UP WI' SAL?"   "AIN'T YER ERD? SHE'S MARRIED AGIN!"

9-1-94

SO VERY CONSIDERATE.

Stout Coster. "WHERE ARE YER GOIN' TO, BILL?"

B·ll. "INTER THE COUNTRY FOR A NICE DRIVE, BEIN' BANK 'OLIDY."

Stout Coster. "SAME 'ERE. I SY! DON'T YER THINK WE MIGHT SWOP MISSESES JUST FOR A FEW HOURS? IT WOULD BE SO MUCH KINDER TO THE HANIMILE!"

4-13-95

"Penny 'Addick."   "Finen?"   "No; thick 'un!"

3-24-94

A SUNDAY DINNER.

Father of Family (who has accidentally shot the leg of a Fowl under the table). "MIND T'DOG DOESN'T GET IT!"
Young Hopeful (triumphantly). "ALL RIGHT, FEYTHER! I'VE GOTTEN ME FOOT ON IT!"

7-27-95

Mother of Amateur Photographer. "WHAT AN IDIOTIC GUY YOU'VE MADE YOUR PAPA LOOK!"
Amateur Photographer. "YES, MAMMA DEAR. BUT *ISN'T* IT *LIKE* HIM?"

5–16–96

'Bus Conductor. "EMMERSMITH! EMMERSMITH! 'ERE YE ARE! EMMERSMITH!"

'Liza Ann. "OO ER YER CALLIN' EMMER SMITH? SORCY 'OUND!"

7–4–96

SONGS AND THEIR SINGERS. No. XV.

Jack (singing at the top of his voice)—
"THERE'S ONLY **ONE** GIRL IN THE WORLD FOR ME!"—*Popular Song.*

9–25–97

Jinks. "I WANT TO BUY A DOG. I DON'T KNOW WHAT THEY CALL THE BREED, BUT IT IS SOMETHING THE SHAPE OF A GREYHOUND, WITH A SHORT, CURLY TAIL AND ROUGH HAIR. DO YOU KEEP DOGS LIKE THAT?" *Fancier.* "NO. I DROWNS 'EM!"

3-19-98

Chemist (to battered female, who is covered with scratches). "THE CAT, I SUPPOSE?"
Battered Female. "NO. ANOTHER LYDY!"

5-21-98

THE "MILK" OF POOR-LAW "KINDNESS."

Jan.–Jun. '43, p. 47

THE FIRST TOOTH.

Jan.–Jun. '43, p. 67

Mr. VANDYKE BROWN, having left the Dress on the Lay Figure carefully arranged, goes out for his usual Exercise, and this is how the Boys took Advantage of his Absence.

Almanack for '65

EUPHEMISM.

Cab Tout (exasperated by the persistent attentions of Constable). "LOOK 'ERE, OLE LIGHTNIN'-KETCHER, W'ERE THE MISSIN' WORD ARE YER SHOVIN' US TO?"

1-7-93

94   Bernard Partridge

MODESTY.

Housewife. "WELL, IF I GIVE YOU SOME BREAKFAST, YOU'LL HAVE TO EARN IT BY CHOPPING SOME WOOD FOR ME."

Tramp. "I'D LIKE TER 'BLIGE YER, LADY. BUT, BLESHYER 'ART, 'TAIN'T FER THE LIKES O' ME TER FOLLER IN THE FOOTSTEPS O' MR. GLADSTONE!"

7-14-94

"THINGS ARE NOT WHAT THEY SEEM."

Mr. Foozler (who, while waiting for the last Train, has wandered to the end of the Platform, opened the door of the Signal-box, and watched the Signalman's manipulations of the levers for some moments with hazy perplexity, suddenly). "Arf o' Burt'n 'n Birrer f' me, Guv'nor!"

3–12–92

"Was he very much cast down after he'd spoken to Papa?"   "Yes. Three Flights of Stairs!"

5–25–95

THE TRUE TEST.

First Screever (stopping before a Pastel in a Picture-dealer's window). "'ULLO, 'ERBERT, LOOK 'ERE! CHALKS!"

Second Screever. "AH, VERY TRICKY, I DESSAY. BUT YOU SET THAT CHAP ON THE PIVEMENT ALONGSIDE O' YOU AN' ME, TO DROR 'ARF A SALMON AN' A NEMPTY 'AT, AN' WHERE 'UD 'E BE?" *First Screever.* "AH!" [*Exeunt ambo.*

7-6-95

Benevolent Old Gentleman. "Now then, little boy. What do you mean by bullying that little girl? Don't you know it's very cruel?"
Rude Little Boy. "Garn! wot's the trouble? She's my sweetheart!"

3-21-96

Tommy (who has just begun learning French, on his first visit to Boulogne). "I SAY, DADDY, DID YOU CALL THAT MAN 'GARÇON'?" *Daddy (with pride).* "YES, MY BOY."

Tommy (after reflection). "I SAY, DADDY, WHAT A BIG GARÇON HE'LL BE WHEN HE'S OUT OF JACKETS AND TURN-DOWNS, AND GETS INTO TAILS AND STICK-UPS!"

8–8–96

NOSCE TEIPSUM.

Lady Cyclist (touring in North Holland). "What a Ridiculous Costume!"

6–4–98

MUSIC-HALL INANITIES. II.

2–8–99

Village Gossip. "Did ye 'ear as owd Sally Sergeant's dead? 'Er what's bin Pew-opener up to Wickleham Church nigh on Fifty Year." *The Village Atheist* (*solemnly*). "Ah! See what comes o' Pew-openin'!"

4-12-99

Papa, Maman, et Bébé s'en vont à la Pêche aux Crevettes.

9-13-99

Desperate Householder writes out advertisement :—"To be disposed of, a Monkey. Very comical and playful. Lively companion ; full of fun. Would exchange for Gold Fish, or anything useful."

10–25–99

THE POINT OF VIEW.

Exasperated Old Gentleman (to Lady in front of him). "Excuse me, Madam, but my Seat has cost me Ten Shillings, and I want to *see*. Your Hat——" *The Lady.* "My Hat has cost me Ten *Guineas*, Sir, and I want it to *be seen!*"

11–8–99

Irish Porter (*thrusting his head into a compartment as the train stops at small, dingy, ill-lit country station*). "Is ᴛʜᴜʀ ᴀɴɴʏʙᴏᴅʏ ᴛʜᴇʀᴇ ꜰᴏʀ *ʜᴇʀᴇ*?"

10-9-1901

Bernard Partridge   103

MAUVAIS SUJET.

Spain. 'CARAMBA! AMIGO JONATHAN, YUUR NEW CITIZEN LOOKS HAPPY!"

Jonathan. "'CITIZEN'! NOT MUCH. GUESS I'LL HAVE TO MAKE A *SUBJECT* OF HIM!'

6-5-1901

BIS DAT QUI CITO DAT.

Lock-keeper (handing ticket). "THREEPENCE, PLEASE."
Little Jenkins. "NOT ME: I'VE JUST PAID THAT FELLOW BACK THERE."
Lock-keeper (drily). "'IM? OH, THAT'S THE CHAP WHO COLLECTS FOR THE BAND!"

8-5-1900

"THALATTA! THALATTA!"

General Chorus (as the Children's Excursion nears its destination). "Oh, I say! There's the Sea! 'Ooray!!'
Small Boy. "I'll be in fust!"

8–8–96

"THEM ARTISES!"

Lady Artist. "Do you belong to that Ship over there?"   *Sailor.* "Yes, Miss."
Lady Artist. "Then would you mind loosening all those Ropes? They are much too tight, and, besides, I can't draw straight lines!"

10–16–97

HYDE PARK, MAY 1.

Country Cousin. "What is the meaning of this, Policeman?"   *Constable.* "Labour Day, Miss."

5-7-98

THE LABOUR MARKET.

Employer. "I shan't speak to you again about getting on with your work, young man. The next time I catch you idling about, you'll have to go."
Boy (confidentially). "Chaps is scarce!"

4-3-1901

A PROPHET IN HIS OWN COUNTRY.

Sylvia. "I wonder whether he'll be a Soldier or a Sailor?"
Mamma. "Wouldn't you like him to be an Artist, like Papa?"
Sylvia. "Oh, One in the Family's quite enough!"

3–8–99

Hedwin. "'Angeleener! Won't yer 'ear me? Wot 'ud yer sy if I told yer as I'd 'took the Shillin' '?" *Hangelina.* "Sy? Why—'Halves'!"

2-21-1900

Leonard Raven-Hill   109

Policeman. "'ERE, CLEAR THIS OUT OF THE WAY."
Little Girl. "GARN WITH YER! YOU WAS IN ONE O' THEM YERSELF ONCE!"

6-27-1900

OUR CHRISTMAS TEA.

Unregenerate Youth. "PASS THE SEEDY CAIKE!"
Vicar's Daughter. "IF?—IF?——"
Unregenerate Youth. "IF 'E DON'T I 'LL SHOVE 'IM IN THE FAICE!

12-25-1901

PREHISTORIC PEEPS.

A Nocturne which would seem to show that "Residential Flats" were not wholly unknown even in Primeval Times!

5–26–94

112   Edward Tennyson Reed

SUCH AN UNEXPECTED PLEASURE!

THE GREAT ADVANTAGE OF HAVING THE ELECTRIC LIGHT "BROUGHT TO YOUR VERY DOOR," WITHOUT ANY PREVIOUS NOTICE, ON THE IDENTICAL DAY, TOO, WHEN YOU ARE GIVING A PARTY, AND YOUR FRIENDS WON'T BE ABLE TO GET WITHIN SOME YARDS OF YOUR HOUSE. AND THEN, SO NICE FOR LADIES IF IT RAINS!

7–12–90

9–6–90

2–24–77

6–24–76

PUNCH'S ESSENCE OF PARLIAMENT

MARCH IL TRIVMPHA·

IRISH MELODIES

MAC DERMOT'S WAR SONG—

WE DONT WANT TO FIGHT BVT BY JINGO IF WE DO WE'VE GOT THE SHIPS WE'VE GOT THE MEN

HONI SOIT QVI MA[L]

LINLEY SAMBOVRNE(?) DEL

UCH cry for three weeks, and mighty little wool now that the "opening day" (*Thursday, January* 17) of the first premature Parliament for eighteen years has come and gone, leaving England a-gape and a-gossip.

Queen's Weather without the QUEEN. In Palace Yard a small crowd, which soon got tired of waiting for celebrities that stole in by other roads than Westminster Hall. Inside the House of Lords, a ha'porth of bread, in the shape of male Peers, to a delightful quantity of sack, in the shape of Ladies. The usual ugly rush of the Commons at the SPEAKER's heels, to the summons of Black Rod—these unmannerly St. Stephen's boys really want another guess sort of rod, applied by Head Master instead of Usher, and by sterner hands than Sir WILLIAM KNOLLYS'; the usual muster of Commissioners in cocked hats and red robes, and the usual more or less distinct reading of a Queen's

1-26-78

Linley Sambourne   115

UNDER THE CENSOR'S STAMP;

Or, how the Bear's Paw comes down on *Punch* in St. Petersburg.   And yet the Jingoes call him "Russophil"!

11-23-78

MR. NARCISSUS RUSKIN.

"Who is it that says most? Which can say more,
Than this rich praise,—that You alone are *You!*"

12–18–80

ANTONIUS TROLLOPIUS.

Author of The Last Chronicles of Cicero.

"O Rare for Antony!"—Shakspeare.

2–5–81

PUNCH'S FANCY PORTRAITS.—No. 37.

"O. W."

"O, I feel just as happy as a bright Sunflower!'
Lays of Christy Minstrelsy.

Æsthete of Æsthetes!
What's in a name?
The poet is Wilde,
But his poetry's tame.

6–25–81

Linley Sambourne   117

CHARLES ROBERT DARWIN, LL.D., F.R.S.

In his *Descent of Man* he brought his own Species down as low as possible—*i.e.*, to "A Hairy Quadruped furnished with a Tail and Pointed Ears, and probably *Arboreal* in its habits"—which is a reason for the very general Interest in a "Family Tree." He has lately been turning his attention to the "Politic Worm."

10–22–81

MR. MATTHEW ARNOLD.

Admit that Homer sometimes nods, that Poets *do* write trash, Our Bard has written "*Balder dead*," and also Balder-dash.

11–26–81

WILKIE COLLINS,

As the Man in White doing Ink-and-Penance for having Written the *Black Robe*.

1–14–82

HERR WAGNER,

THE BI-CYCLE-IST OF HER MAJESTY'S AND DRURY LANE.

5-6-82

H. M. STANLEY.

PORTRAIT OF THE EXPLORER LOOKING OUT FOR M. DE BRAZZA. "I'LL
LET HIM KNOW IF HE CON-GO ON LIKE THIS!"

"So have I heard on Afric's burning shore
Another Lion give a grievous roar,
And the first Lion thought the last a bore."
From that classic "Bombastes Furioso."

10-28-82

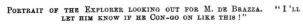

ABBÉ FRANZ LIZST.

ABBÉ THOUGHT (OF COURSE).—"LIZST, LIZST, O LIZST!"

11-3-83

Linley Sambourne　119

CHRISTMAS WAITS.

Trio. "Oh, Bless you, Gentlemen, whose looks
Are very far from frowning,
Pay cash, and buy the latest books
Of Tennyson, Swinburne, Browning!"

12–27–84

PUNCH'S ALMANACK FOR 1885.

"THE SANDS OF CHRONOS."

Almanack for '85

Linley Sambourne

THE WELSH HARPOONIST.

THE RETURN OF WILLIAM THE WHALER FROM AN ATTEMPT AT CATCHING WALES DURING
THE RECESS.

6–11–87

OUR AFGHAN "BOUNDARY COMMISSION." JOHN BULL PUTS UP A NOTICE. (*See p.* 105.)

2-28-85

THE OSPREY AND THE EAGLES.

"The abdication of King MILAN of Servia .... has at length fallen like a thunderbolt on the State-craft of Europe."—*Times*.

FALLEN at last, but not *quite* like a thunderbolt!
  Osprey is hardly a Jovian bird;
Rather a fowl that will, after big blunder, bolt;
  Timid rapacity's slightly absurd.

True birds of prey should be boldly belligerent,
  Dauntless in danger, and strong on the wing;
Crises on cocktails will act as refrigerant,
  Courage he needs who of air would be king.

3-16-89

NEW KING COAL.

(A new Mining-Capitalist Version of an old Nursery Rhyme, dedicated and commended to the thoughtful consideration of the colliers on strike in Northumberland and Durham.)

Linley Sambourne.

[PUTTING it in the form of a conundrum, *Mr. Punch* would ask the Colliers who may read this rhyme the following question, the answer to which may throw a light upon the meaning of New King COAL's jubilant doggerel ditty:—

"When prices rise—even in the midst of the Dog Days—and the output of first-class coal falls, who reaps the advantage of the enhanced value and readier sale of accumulated stocks of small and slaggy 'rubbish'?"]

O our New King COAL
Is an artful old soul,
    And an artful old soul is he;
And a jolly good Strike
Is a game he must like—
    When it pulls in the £ *s. d.*

8-19-93

" BOUND FOR THE BALTIC SEA!'

[Mr. GLADSTONE starts for a trip to the Baltic in the Donald Currie Ship *Tantallon Castle*, Wednesday, June 12.]

6–15–95

Almanack for '51

Almanack for '63

"NEW CROWNS FOR OLD ONES!"

(ALADDIN *adapted.*)

4–15–76

John Tenniel   129

THE PIG AND THE PEASANT.

PEASANT. "AH! I'D LIKE TO BE CARED VOR HALF AS WELL AS THEE BE!"

9–19–63

A LESSON.

3-1-79

John Tenniel   131

DROPPING THE PILOT.
3-29-90

CAPTAIN JINKS (OF THE "SELFISH") AND HIS FRIENDS ENJOYING THEMSELVES ON THE RIVER.

8-21-69